Lucia Mthiyane

Kitchen Queen

*For my mother Catherine,
the most beautiful woman in the world,
who taught me to follow my dreams.*

First published in 2020 by Human & Rousseau (2020)
an imprint of NB Publishers
A division of Media24 Boeke (Pty) Ltd
40 Heerengracht, Cape Town 8001

Copyright © published edition: Human & Rousseau (2020)
Copyright © text: Lucia Mthiyane (2020)

No part of this book may be reproduced or transmitted in any form or by any electronic or mechanical means, including photocopying and recording, or by any other information storage or retrieval system, without written permission from the publisher.

Publisher: Lindy Samery
Editor: Nelani Pfaff
Proofreader: Glynne Newlands
Designer: Wilna Combrinck
Photographer: Henk Hattingh
Illustrations and styling: Hannes Koegelenberg
Food preparation: Tani Kirsten
Index: Nelani Pfaff

Printed by novus print, a division of Novus Holdings

ISBN: 978-0-7981-8003-0

DISCLAIMER: The information and advice shared in this book is not intended as a substitute for the skincare and/or medical advice of your dermatologist / skincare specialist, doctor and/or physician. The author and the publisher do not assume and hereby disclaim any liability to any party for any loss, damage or disruption caused by errors or omissions, whether such errors or omissions result from negligence, accident, or any other cause. The reader should consult a medical / skincare practitioner with respect to any symptoms that may require diagnosis or medical attention prior to following any advice given in this book.

Contents

ONCE UPON A TIME 5
WHAT'S IN A NAME 6
MEMORIES, MILESTONES AND MAINSTAY RECIPES 7
REMEMBER THE MICROWAVE? 8
HAPPINESS IS HOME-MADE 12
FROM CAREER COMPROMISES TO COOKING CLASSES 24
SOCIAL MEDIA'S ROLE IN MY REPERTOIRE OF RECIPES 25

Pantry Staples 27
The Food I Grew to Love 41
Seven Colours 61
Curry Queen 77
Maize Starz 97
Meat Mains, Roasts and Sides 113
Outdoor and Picnic Food 137
Cakes, Bakes and Puddings 153
Food for Body and Soul 169

ACKNOWLEDGEMENTS 188
INDEX 190

"Once upon a time ...

" ... there was this girl. She was bold, and brave, and daring. Her family knew this from the moment she was born. With her first cry she announced to the world that she would shine as bright as her smile with which she could light up the deepest, darkest night sky. Her eyes were pure and filled with specks of stardust. In her heart she carried hope and dreams and determination. It rushed through her veins like the thunderous Umzinyathi River, the first force of nature other than herself that she became aware of.

The place she would call home was named after the river that runs through it: Umzinyathi, just north of Durban, in KwaZulu-Natal, one of South Africa's most luscious regions. This river, the largest tributary of the Tugela River, set the scene in which this little girl would one day become a queen. Just like the source of the Tugela in Majuba Hill – The Hill of Doves – she knew she had the wings of a thousand doves with which one day she would reach her highest goals. Everyone who laid eyes on her in those very first moments when her life began, saw the light inside her, and they called her Lucia – which means: Graceful Light."

This is where I started from. Lo and behold, no fairy tale. I have worked hard to fuel my own fire and to make my dreams come true: actress, model, jazz singer, entrepreneur, but most important of all: self-made kitchen queen. For the past ten years in the food industry, I have had a culinary journey as colourful as the strong foundation upon which I have built my whole life and my career as celebrity chef. Without the cornerstones of family, food, tradition and home – Umzinyathi – I would not have been ready to fill these pages with my story, my memories, and my culinary creations.

Within these pages you will find my secret to success: passion, purpose, preparation, persistence in pursuing the process until I reach perfection ...

Within these pages you will find me, the Kitchen Queen as my friends and followers call me. And you will find my food infused with flavour and flair, enthused with love and light and grace. I try to carry grace and light into everything I touch, and I hope that you see it shining through this book that I have waited so long to share with all of you.

"What's in a name ..."

Often the meaning behind a name has a significant impact on the bearer. My ultimate goal in life is to be a Graceful Light in this world, and thus far it has served me well.

Arriving at a name for my cookbook took some time. In the end I realised that most of life's answers do not lie in the "what" but in the "why". With every new endeavour, we not only need to ask ourselves what it is, or what we will call it, but also why we are creating it. And then we need to answer ourselves truthfully.

Food is a sharing, caring, daring medium to work with. I love it! I am passionate about the process and enthusiastic about the culinary experiences I create. Of all the fields in which I have furthered myself and of all the mediums I have worked with, from being an actress and singer on stage to being a model and influencer on real and virtual pages, making my voice heard on television and radio, through my online blogs and social media, as food editor of a magazine to partnering with big brands and spreading my entrepreneurial wings, the single most rewarding and thrilling of all my endeavours thus far has been transforming myself into a self-taught celebrity chef. Today I am a self-made foodie and I love taking the everyday ordinary and elevating it to the extraordinary. So when one of my followers called me the Queen of the Kitchen in a comment on social media, something rang true and resonated in me. From that moment the name *Kitchen Queen* just kind of stuck.

From preparing feasts to teaching cooking classes, I have found the absolute best way to express myself is through food. I value quality and I not only infuse my heart and soul into all of my meticulously designed dishes, but I strive to enthuse love and light and grace into each and every one of my creations. Each bite must lift your spirit. You must be able to taste the inspiration and joy that went into preparing it. I want my food to excite and enthral, and in order to achieve this goal, I want to create food that will make you want to embrace life with an enthusiasm that spills over into the lives of others. After all, we are all influencers in our own way. And we can all be the kings and queens of our kitchens.

Memories, Milestones and Mainstay Recipes

My fondest food memories ...

Food has always been an important part of my life. I come from a family and extended family who truly loves good food. My paternal grandparents had a vast piece of land in Umzinyathi, north of Durban, in KwaZulu-Natal. They were the proud producers of the most delicious fruit and vegetables – apples, oranges, grapes, mangoes, avocados, berries, pumpkin, sweet potatoes, madumbes *(yams) ...*

I clearly remember the bags in which they kept the beans, maize and nuts. Oh, and the mischief we got ourselves into with those bags and bags of nuts. They were actually kept in what could be more accurately described as a sack. In my mind's eye I can still see the room in which these sacks were kept. My cousins and I would sneak in and steal the nuts by breaking the sack open from the bottom, and when we had eaten our way halfway through the sack, we would start on another one from the bottom. We got into so much trouble, but it was so much fun!

When my mom quit teaching to study at university, my older sisters decided that a good way to earn money was to sell sandwiches at my school. They would give the sandwiches a filling made of tinned fish, and then I was roped in to sell them at school. But I really liked these sandwiches and most of the time I ended up eating most of them myself. What an entrepreneur I was!

As a child, Sunday was my favourite day. It was filled to the brim with a sense of belonging, family, fun and food. From the moment we woke up to get dressed to go to church we were excited. Excited to feel the spirit and the music fill your soul. Excited to hear so many voices come together in perfect harmony. And extremely excited about the seven-colour Sunday lunch! My earliest memories always take me back to these moments in which I believe my fascination with and appreciation of good music, good company and good food started. And as I reminisce, I realise how solid the foundation of every aspect of my career was laid in these moments.

Remember the microwave?

Another wow-moment came the day the microwave oven arrived! My mother was one of the first people in our neighbourhood to own a microwave, and this brings back so many happy memories. I can still taste her special microwave chicken dish which became one of our favourites. Just the other day I was talking to my sister about our favourite food while growing up, and she reminded me that our microwave doubled up as a convection oven – this made cooking even easier. No wonder I was so fascinated by this appliance! As siblings, the five of us used to take turns to cook our family's meals. It wasn't exactly a chore we all enjoyed, especially not for one of my sisters, until the microwave arrived and became the focal point in my mother's kitchen. Today my sister still does not enjoy cooking as much as I do. She cooks almost only once a year and that's on Christmas Day. But for me, this legendary old microwave created many a fond memory.

Soon after purchasing the microwave/convection oven, Mom bought a microwave cookbook that opened up a world of new dishes to try out. Thereafter we cooked just about anything and everything in the microwave, because we came to realise that if approached correctly, the microwave had a solution for just about everything. Want to scramble an egg, but without the hassle of using the stove and a pan and cleaning up? Beat the egg in a bowl, pop it in the microwave and eat it straight out of the dish it's in! Tired of burning any starch: pap, pasta, rice, potatoes? Pop it in just enough water in the microwave! Hate soggy vegetables cooked beyond death? Startle-steam them in the microwave so that they still have just the right amount of crunch when you bite into them!

Using the microwave became such a huge part of our daily lives that we actually started referring to it as a member of the family. My sister is pretty sure we still have that same old microwave back home. So more than four decades along the line, the microwave literally became part of the furniture.

Even as a chef and kitchen queen, I sometimes still turn to my good old friend The Microwave. To this day there is one microwave recipe in particular that I swear by. It gives you a great alternative if you are not a fan of greens, like spinach. After so many years, I find it surprising that it keeps on being one of my favourite side dishes! See my recipe for Microwave Greens on page 10.

Microwave Greens

As a child – like most children – I hated green vegetables in any shape, size and form. Especially if they were overcooked. And yet, isn't it funny how leafy greens have now suddenly become so trendy, even among children if they are taught to appreciate the crunch!

Serves 4–6

280 g tender-stem broccoli
100 g mini-asparagus
150 g fine green beans, tops trimmed
6 baby marrows, halved lengthways
micro-greens or herbs, to garnish
melted butter, to drizzle over
freshly squeezed lemon juice

1. Place all the vegetables into a shallow microwavable dish.
2. Add only a little bit of water to cover the vegetables.
3. Cover the dish with cling film. Use a sharp knife to pierce four small holes in the cling film.
4. Microwave on high for 3 to 4 minutes. The vegetables should still be bright green and slightly crunchy.
5. Garnish with fresh micro-greens or herbs, drizzle with the melted butter and add a dash of lemon juice as the final touch.

Happiness is Home-Made

As I grew older, I began to appreciate the process of cooking and baking more and more. I started experimenting with different ingredients, and my mother allowed me these culinary adventures. To this day, I thank her for instilling in me a love of good food, because it takes time and hard work to cultivate an appreciation for anything worthy of being appreciated in life. My happy place is my kitchen – my creative castle where I have worked hard to be the queen. My plates are my canvas and I paint colourful landscapes with food. I conjure fragrances and flavours. I combine sight, smell and taste, and then I savour the moment when I realise it all works well together.

One of the things that my mother taught me to appreciate is something so basic that it took me many years before I grasped the reason why. Mom loved home-made bread! I never completely understood why until later in life. I always asked myself why anyone would bake his or her own bread. It takes so much time and effort, and it is way more expensive than store-bought bread. So why go through all that trouble if you can rather pop into a shop and buy a much cheaper loaf? But now I understand. By being able to bake the most basic bread, you can meet your own most basic need – to feed. And even kitchen queens need to eat!

My mother taught me that no store-bought bread compares to home-made bread. And that nothing makes a house feel like a home more than the smell of bread baking in the oven. But most of all, she taught me that happiness is home-made.

Steamed or Baked Bread

Now that you know the story behind my "Home-Made Bread" Life Lesson, you also know why we never ate store-bought bread, but you might be wondering how we managed to always have freshly baked bread at home ... My mother is a marvellous woman, and much like our dear old microwave, she always has a solution for every problem. Therefore, she instructed that the five siblings had to take turns to bake bread. Problem solved!

The following recipe can be used to make steamed bread or home-baked bread. The only difference between the two is that steamed bread is cooked in a large pot on a stove, whereas the baked bread is baked in an oven.

Steamed bread, affectionately known as ujeqe in isiZulu, is a staple in most homes in KwaZulu-Natal. In Gauteng they call it idombolo (dumpling). The KZN version of this dumpling usually accompanies a cooked stew, or more accurately is cooked in the stew. It is very easy to make. You simply mix self-raising flour with warm water and salt, then add the mixture into the cooked stew, and you end up with a kind of one-pot wonder.

Maize Meal and Flour Bread

This bread is tasty on its own or with butter. It makes great sandwiches, and it is the ideal side for curries and stews. Or enjoy it for breakfast with a cup of tea. It keeps well in the freezer for up to a month. However, do not defrost it in the microwave. Rather take it out of the freezer the night before and let it defrost at room temperature.

Makes 1 loaf of bread
Serves 4

500 ml cold water, to place in oven while preheating

30 ml sugar
400 ml warm water
15 g (1½ sachet) dry yeast
2 ml honey (optional)
45 g butter, melted
15 ml salt
750 g bread flour
250 g maize meal

1. Preheat the oven to 180 °C. To help the bread to rise, pour the cold water in a skillet and place it in the oven while preheating.
2. In a large bowl, dissolve the sugar in the warm water, and stir in the yeast. The yeast will proof within 5 minutes. To help the yeast to proof, add the honey.
3. Add the melted butter and salt, then add the flour and maize meal, and knead for about 7 minutes if using an electric mixer, or 10 to 11 minutes if kneading with your hands. Add more water if the dough is too stiff.
4. Cover the bowl with cling wrap and let it proof in a warm place for 45 minutes to an hour. You may proof your dough in the oven, just make sure that the oven is turned off and not hot.
5. Punch the dough down and divide between two 20-cm greased loaf tins. Cover and let the dough rise again until it has doubled in size.
6. Bake at 180 °C for 30 minutes.
7. Once cooked, it will be golden on top. Flip it over and keep it wrapped in a damp cloth. Let it rest for about 20 minutes before serving.

My Pasta Debut

The very first recipe I ever came up with on my own was a pasta dish made with pasta screws and pork sausages wrapped in bacon. I still remember it as if it was yesterday. Heaven knows how I invented such a complex recipe in the 1980s! I possibly saw it in a magazine ... I tell you, it was quite a sight. My cousin Thula remarked, "You are cooking as if today is your last day on earth!".

Pasta with Bacon-Wrapped Pork Bangers

Ideal as an easy dinner during the week, or for brunch. Remember: It is important to soak the toothpicks beforehand to prevent them burning while you roast the sausages.

Serves 4

toothpicks, soaked in water

25 ml vegetable oil
8 pork bangers
200 g or 8 rashers of streaky bacon
extra oil, to drizzle
250 g pasta screws, cooked according to packet instructions
250 ml of Lucia's Béchamel Sauce (see page 18)
roasted tomatoes and fresh basil, to serve

1. Preheat the oven to 180 °C.
2. Heat a large non-stick pan and add the oil. (Alternatively, roast the bangers in the oven from the start and skip steps 2 and 3.)
3. Cook over medium to high heat for about 5 minutes, ensuring that all sides are properly cooked.
4. Wrap each sausage with bacon. Use toothpicks to secure and hold the bacon in place.
5. Line an oven tray with baking paper. Place the bacon-wrapped sausages on the tray and drizzle with oil.
6. Roast in the preheated oven for about 15 minutes.
7. Once cooked, set aside and take the toothpicks out.
8. In a serving dish, add the béchamel sauce to the pasta. Mix until well combined. Add the sausages and serve with roasted tomatoes and fresh basil.

Lucia's Béchamel Sauce

Makes ±500 ml

425 ml milk
5 black peppercorns
1 bay leaf
1 slice of onion, 5 mm thick
1 sprig parsley
40 g butter
20 g plain flour
salt and pepper, to taste

1. Pour the milk into a small saucepan and set over low heat.
2. Add the peppercorns, bay leaf, onion and parsley to the milk.
3. Let it simmer for about 5 minutes.
4. Remove the saucepan from the stove and strain the milk into a small jug.
5. Using the same pan, melt the butter and then add the flour while stirring to form a smooth paste.
6. Add the flavoured milk bit by bit, stirring continuously with a whisk while cooking over low heat. This will ensure a smooth, creamy, silky sauce.
7. Turn the heat down and simmer over low heat for 5 minutes while whisking at intervals.
8. Add salt and pepper, and stir through.
9. Pour the sauce into a jug and place cling wrap directly on top of the sauce to prevent skin forming on the surface.
10. Keep the jug in a medium-sized pot with warm water until needed.

My Go-To Fish Dish

We all need a curry-in-a-hurry quick and easy recipe we can make a day or two in advance. When you know you are in for a busy week, make sure there is enough left over, because if refrigerated this dish can keep well up to a week.

When using tinned fish, I really do not bother cleaning it by taking the bones out. These bones are so soft and flaky that by the end of the cooking process, you will hardly be able to detect them by focussing on texture.

I prefer to use two cans of tinned fish at a time, because this dish is even more delicious the next day. You can also use it in or on snacks, as a filling for toasted sandwiches, or to create lunchbox surprises for your family.

Tinned Fish Curry

Tinned fish is packed with omega 3, so bulk up on it. Add peas if you like, because it not only adds colour and flavour, but it also stretches the dish even further.

Serves 6

40 g butter or ghee
10 ml vegetable oil
1 onion, cut into thin slices
10 fresh curry leaves, chopped
1 sprig thyme
15 ml ginger and garlic paste
10 ml turmeric
20 ml curry powder of your choice
salt and pepper, to taste
1 medium tomato, peeled and diced
5 ml tomato paste
2 cans of tinned fish (e.g. pilchards or sardines)
6 eggs
chopped fresh coriander, to garnish
cooked basmati rice, to serve

1. In a hot skillet, melt the butter and oil together over moderate heat.
2. Sauté the onion and then add the curry leaves, thyme, ginger and garlic paste, turmeric and curry powder. Stir well to combine.
3. Add salt and pepper, and stir through.
4. Add the tomato and tomato paste, and stir through.
5. Add a splash of water if anything starts sticking to the bottom of the skillet, and stir.
6. Add the fish and cover with the sauce – make sure not to break the fish.
7. Carefully break in the eggs and cover, cooking over low heat for 5 minutes, depending on how you like your eggs.
8. Garnish with coriander and serve with basmati rice.

Family First

Leg of lamb is one of those sacred family dishes that I enjoy making. It always brings back precious family memories, and time after time it succeeds in creating even more special moments, shared with much love. One day when my mom visited me in Jo'burg, I prepared leg of lamb in a slow cooker served with mixed seasonal vegetables, but with a bit of a twist of apples. My mom truly enjoyed that dish, and afterwards she always asked me to cook it for her whenever I visited Durban.

Leg of Lamb with Apples

This is a firm family favourite. As mentioned above, I prepared this dish for my mom and on a whim I added apple to the roasted seasonal veg.

Serves 8–10

leg of lamb, weighing ±2,5 kg
4 cloves of garlic, peeled
2 sprigs rosemary
15 ml vegetable oil
2 carrots, cut into large chunks
1 onion, cut into quarters
4 red apples, cored and quartered
150 ml red wine
250 ml beef stock

1. Preheat the oven to 180 °C.
2. Rub the lamb with the garlic and rosemary.
3. Use a sharp pointed knife and make at least 30 small incisions all over the meat. Thinly slice the garlic cloves you used to rub the meat, and put a slice into each incision. Reserve some garlic to add to the dish with the vegetables later on.
4. Pull off small springs of rosemary and push into the incisions.
5. Cover the lamb well and refrigerate for an hour.
6. Remove from the fridge 1 hour before roasting. The meat must be at room temperature.
7. Grease a large roasting tin with the oil.
8. Scatter the remaining garlic and rosemary together with the carrots, onion and apples over the bottom of the roasting tin.
9. Pour the wine and stock over, and then place the lamb on a wire rack in the roasting tin.
10. Cover with foil and roast for about 1½ hours.
11. Turn the lamb over halfway through the cooking time.
12. Turn the oven grill on and grill the lamb for 10 minutes.
13. When cooked, remove the roast from the oven and allow it to rest, still covered, in a warm place, for about 30 minutes.
14. Serve with lamb gravy and roast potatoes.

From Career Compromises to Cooking Classes

Initially I wanted to study speech and drama at university, but my grades were not good enough and I was not accepted to the course – a story for another day … I later graduated as a teacher from college with distinctions, for which I am very thankful. Another achievement of which I am very proud, is that I was selected to represent South Africa at Eagling College, London, together with nine other English teachers, to receive training in new, advanced methods of teaching English at high school level.

When you are young and life just happens as it happens, you get discouraged, but thank God for my mother Catherine who was a teacher herself. She encouraged me to obtain my Teacher Training Diploma, and later this would prove immensely helpful when I started conducting cooking classes. These eventually became a big hit all over the country. I went on to teach for seven years, and relocated from Durban to Johannesburg with the intention of pursuing my acting and singing career. I started teaching at a school in Braamfontein until the school closed and left me very disappointed – little did I know then that it was a blessing in disguise.

I started acting and singing part-time. Monyeen Lee, my agent arranged my first TV commercial for Bears Furniture as well as an audition for a part in the theatre musical *Girl Talk*, with Richard Loring. I got the part and the musical ran for 13 months. This experience opened many doors for me in the corporate entertainment industry. Felicia Mabuza Suttle invited us to her talk show and we performed all the hits from the musical. And then fame struck, let me tell you!

But deep down I always knew my greatest passion was food, and so did all the girls who performed with me as well as the band. I hold these people near and dear to my heart, because they always encouraged me to pursue my dream of cooking for crowds.

So through the years I kept my dream alive while I made many career moves. I shared my vision with my family, friends and colleagues, and I am so grateful for the support and encouragement they gave me. This book you are holding in your hands has always been on the back-burner in my head. Over time I have come up with hundreds of recipes. I have tried and tested them on my family, friends and even strangers.

I have tried to simplify them so that they are enjoyable and can be shared further. Over the years I have come to enjoy cooking various curries, be it lamb, beef, pork, seafood or vegetables. When it comes to spices, I combine, mix and layer my own spices. Once packaged, I share them with family and friends who also love to cook. I have even started producing my own range of condiments.

One of my closest friends, Thobile Gebashe, swears by the simple tricks I taught her many moons ago. Thobile and many other people who have attended my cooking classes continue to follow me on social media. At first I only conducted the cooking classes periodically, but they have become very popular. I still remember my very first class in 2011: I had 12 attendees at a supermarket kitchen studio in Hurlingham. This first intimate class made me realise that there was a gap in the market. These folks were sick and tired of cooking the same old dishes day in and day out. They craved something new, something exciting and challenging at the same time. I started travelling to all our major cities – Cape Town, Durban, Bloemfontein, Mpumalanga, Mafikeng – to conduct cooking classes, and these classes were an instant hit all-over. A friend suggested that I incorporate White Star Super Maize

Meal, and so I started on a wonderful journey with them. White Star Super Maize Meal eventually partnered with me to use their product in my classes. However, to be honest, maize meal was never my or my mother's favourite. I remember one time when I was about five years old, I was craving *amasi* (sour milk) and my mama made me *amasi* using rice because I wouldn't eat *uphuthu* (dry *pap*).

I came up with dozens of maize meal recipes, after testing and tasting them. A booklet was compiled and the recipes became part of the White Star Super Maize Meal classes, which were popular for more than seven years. In 2012, White Star Super Maize Meal also launched a new product: White Star Quick. I became part of the team who travelled throughout South Africa to introduce this new product, and it was on these tours that I was able to combine all of my talents – singing, acting and cooking demonstrations – to entertain crowds. We had so much fun! And then, a few years down the line, a new product, instant porridge, became a hit as a result of cooking demonstrations that I did live on *The Morning Show* on e.TV.

Cooking and sharing my knowledge in my cooking classes has brought me some of the proudest moments in my life. So let me share with you one of my favourite tricks to teach ...

Social Media's Role in my Repertoire of Recipes

My career has taken many a turn and I have worked in various fields with a variety of mediums, but none as powerful as social media. Social media and word of mouth are two incredibly influential tools when you are trying to make your mark in any industry. Whenever I post pictures of my dishes on social media platforms, my followers always ask for the recipes and I'm always happy to share them. I have a growing following on Instagram, Twitter and Facebook, and I am so humbled by the idea that all these people find what I have to share useful and worthy of incorporating into their lives. It is an honour and a privilege to be deemed an influencer. This has led to many food brands wanting to collaborate with me. I am often asked to come up with unconventional recipes, sometimes in collaboration with other chefs as well. Whether I develop recipes on my own or together with other foodies, it is one of the most rewarding creative processes to experience.

In essence this book was born out of all the loves, likes and shares I have received from fans. Thank you for your support and enthusiasm. Thank you for sharing my love for good food. Thank you for appreciating the stories behind my dishes.

After reading this intro, I think you can already tell that this is no ordinary cookbook. This is not only a collection of recipes, but also a compilation of memories that I hold near and dear to my heart. I have found the secret to changing everyday dishes into extraordinary taste sensations. It is a secret so simple and serendipitous that it makes this Zulu girl feel like a queen ... a Kitchen Queen! I have learned that the best building blocks in cooking and baking remains the basics. And when you build on those basics, the secrets unfold all by themselves. So, come and take a peek in my pantry ...

Pantry Staples

The staples I stock in my kitchen cupboard are not at all fancy, but I consider them essential. Most of them are typical ingredients you will find in any supermarket, so these products are readily available, but their presence versus their absence can make or break almost any dish. It's as simple as that.

When we talk about pantry staples, we usually think about dry, long-life, canned, bottled and preserved ingredients. However, I have a few equally important refrigerated staples, and the make-or-break rule applies to them too.

And then, of course, I do have a few favourites that can be classified as key ingredients or secrets. Wonderful condiments and spices that, much like a catchy melody or some vocal loops, ensure a musical composition so enticing, it justifies the need to become lyrical about the taste sensations they create. Since I am originally from Durban, I seem to lean towards heat, if you know what I mean. Almost every savoury meal I prepare must have a bit of a kick. I even have my own range of chilli sauces, curry mixes and I grow my own bird's eye chilli bush. In this chapter, I have arranged the basic essentials that relate to the other chapters and recipes in this book. I absolutely cannot cook without having these ingredients available.

My bare minimum:
onion powder
salt and pepper
vegetable/canola oil

For curries and stews:
my best basic curry mix (see page 35)
masala mixes (see page 34)
garlic and ginger
turmeric
tomato paste
garam masala
fennel seeds
mustard seeds
star anise

Other staples at room temperature:
flour
eggs
cornflour (for thickening)
yeast
gelatine powder
breadcrumbs or panko
maize/*pap*
basmati rice
jasmine rice
pasta rice
beans (tinned and dry)
tinned tomatoes
sesame seeds
sauces
honey
Lucia's Chilli Sauce (see page 33)

Refrigerated staples:
beef stock (see page 38)
butter or ghee
amasi (sour cream)
plain yoghurt
fresh cream
variety of fresh herbs

For roasts:
soy sauce
red wine vinegar
apple cider vinegar
extra virgin olive oil
white and red wine
sherry
honey
Worcestershire sauce

For pastas:
variety of pasta
tomato sauce (see page 30)
tomato paste
long-life creams

For baking:
brown sugar
white sugar
icing sugar
castor sugar
cocoa
dark chocolate
condensed milk
baking powder
vanilla extract or paste
self-raising flour

Spices and herbs:
ground coriander
peppercorns
dried rosemary
dried thyme
dried oregano
dried parsley
curry leaves
dried mixed herbs

Lucia's Tomato Sauce

We all love tomato sauce. Especially children! But think about all the preservatives and the loads of sugar the manufacturers add to it ... If you make your own, you have control over the ingredients you choose to put into it. This recipe makes an extraordinary, tasty tomato sauce – truly delicious with fries, in pasta, on pizza and just about anything and everything else. So, if you have the time, make your own tomato sauce. Believe me, you will be proud of your product, and you can even package it as gifts for family and friends.

Makes ±300 ml

1 kg ripe tomatoes
30 ml sugar (brown or white)
45 ml vegetable oil
1 onion, peeled and diced
5 ml crushed garlic
salt and pepper, to taste
15 ml chopped fresh basil
15 ml chopped fresh oregano
juice of 1 lemon

1. Bring a medium sized saucepan of water to the boil. Add the tomatoes and boil for 2 minutes. Remove the tomatoes and place into a bowl with cold water and set aside for 5 minutes to cool.
2. When cool enough, peel the tomatoes. Cut them in half and remove the seeds. Finely chop them and sprinkle with sugar. Set aside. You will add them later to make the sauce.
3. In a large pan, heat the oil and sauté the onion until translucent.
4. Add the garlic, salt and pepper, and cook while stirring for 2 minutes.
5. Add the tomatoes and stir through. Add the basil and oregano. Let it cook over high heat at first, then reduce the heat, and simmer uncovered for about 2 hours, or until the sauce becomes a paste and all the water has evaporated. Keep stirring so that the sauce does not burn.
6. Decant the cooked sauce into a large bowl and let it cool. Then add the lemon juice and stir through.
7. Bottle the tomato sauce in sterilised jars, or use freezer jars if you plan on freezing it.

Lucia's Chilli Sauce (Jalapeño)

As I have said before, I love heat in my food. You will not believe how serious I am about this! I take a tub of my own home-made chilli sauce with me everywhere I go. When I recently went to Greece on holiday, my friends were shocked when they found out that I took a tub of my chilli sauce with me. But for the rest of the two weeks that we were there, the secret tub of chilli sauce became part of all our meals. What I love about my chilli sauce is that I can control the heat and the sweetness.

Makes 500 ml

125 ml vegetable oil
15 ml crushed garlic
1 onion, roughly chopped
4–6 medium jalapeños, deseeded if you do not want too much heat
salt and pepper, to taste
15 ml Dry Masala Powder Mix (see page 36)
4 tomatoes, peeled and chopped
15 ml lemon or lime juice
5 ml sugar

1. Place all the ingredients, except the lemon or lime juice and sugar, in a food processor and blend until combined.
2. Transfer the mix to a small saucepan and bring to a simmer while stirring for about 5 minutes.
3. Add the lemon or lime juice, as well as the sugar. Stir until the sugar has dissolved.
4. Allow to cool slightly.
5. Bottle the sauce in sterilised jars.

Masala Mixes

Anybody who knows me well, knows that I am all about adding spice to life, and I am passionate about spicy food too! There is this shop in Jo'burg where I used to buy all my Indian delicacies, especially a wet masala that was sold in a plastic container for R30 each. The rich red colour of the mix attracted me, because it held the promise that adding it to any curry would be absolutely divine. I bought myself a tub and the rest is history.

After being a loyal customer for many years, the thought crossed my mind that surely I could try to make my own version of this wet masala. I came up with a recipe and at first I sold it only among my friends, but the product became so popular that I extended it into a whole range of my own masala mixes. The manufacturing of these mixes soon grew into a booming business beyond our borders, and I now have customers who send through their orders from as far as Botswana and Swaziland.

My wet and dry masala mixes (recipes on page 36) are part of my kitchen staples. They form the foundation of all my curries and stews. When I prepare big batches, I keep them in the freezer – they keep well for up to six months. Just ensure you take it out of the freezer the night before you would like to use it.

My Best Basic Curry Mix

To make a decent curry, you need to get the basics right. Start with:

masala, which consists of:

20 ml garam masala
5 ml turmeric
2,5 ml fennel seeds
2,5 ml mustard seeds
1 star anise
3 cardamom pods
1 bay leaf
5 ml chill flakes

... then add:

5 ml grated ginger
5 ml crushed garlic
30 ml plain yoghurt
15 ml fresh cream, and
2,5 ml honey

... and off you go!

Wet Masala Paste Mix

For the dry spices, it is easier to purchase them in quantities measured in grams.

Makes ±250 ml

30 ml finely chopped fresh garlic
20 ml finely chopped fresh ginger
20 g ground cumin
25 g ground coriander
125 g finely chopped onion
20 g garam masala
20 g red chilli powder
20 g paprika
200 g unsweetened dry coconut
water, as needed

1. Place all the ingredients in a food processor or blender, and process into a fine paste. Add water if needed.
2. Keep the paste in an airtight container.
3. It keeps longer in a cool place or fridge.

Dry Masala Powder Mix

You can double or triple the recipe and make a huge batch that will last you quite a while.

Makes ±300 g

2 cinnamon sticks
30 g cloves
5 bay leaves
40 g dried chilli flakes
1 medium nutmeg, grated OR 5 g ground nutmeg
50 g green cardamom pods
80 g cumin seeds
40 g coriander seeds
40 g black peppercorns

1. Roast all the ingredients together in a dry pan over moderate heat – do not let them burn.
2. Let it cool down, then process in a food processor to form a fine powder.
3. Transfer the powder into an airtight container. It can be stored like this for up to two months.

Wet Masala Paste Mix

Dry Masala Powder Mix

Lucia's Beef Stock

It is important that you use beef bones and meat scraps for this stock, so make the effort of sourcing the best from your local butcher or supermarket.

Makes ±750 ml

vegetable oil, for frying
1 kg beef bones and meat scraps
1 medium onion, roughly chopped
2 celery sticks, chopped
2 cloves of garlic
2 carrots, roughly chopped
30 ml finely chopped fresh parsley
15 ml peppercorns
2 litres boiling water

1. In a large pot, heat the oil and fry the bones and meat scraps while continually tossing.
2. Add the onion, celery and garlic. Sauté until the bones and meat scraps are thoroughly browned.
3. Add the carrots, parsley and peppercorns. Stir through. Then slowly add the boiling water while stirring.
4. Cook the stock uncovered over low heat and let it simmer until it has reduced to about 750 ml (3 cups) – this will take about 3 hours.
5. Once cooked, set aside to cool slightly and then strain through a sieve.
6. Once completely cooled, pour it into a jar and store it in the fridge. It will have a layer of fat, so discard the fat using a spoon before you use the stock.

The Food I Grew To Love

Many of us have food pet hates we develop over time, and often it started when we were little. Perhaps it is something your parents always insisted you eat, or maybe you were horrified by how foreign and strange it looked that there simply was no way of persuading you to try it. For me, it comes down to a combination of things of which I have no fond food memories. Sometimes it was an ingredient that formed part of a dish, which might not have been prepared well. Either way, I think we should keep an open mind when it comes to food. These days I try not to say, "No, I don't eat that." I try to let go of my preconceived notions. So when presented with something that I had always thought I disliked, I look at it as part of a new dish. More often than not I am pleasantly surprised to then find I end up loving it.

As an artist and musician, I am constantly exposed to different genres of music, but we all know that as a child you had no choice in the matter and had to listen to the music your parents decided to play in their home. When you move away from home, you inevitably will be exposed to new music and learn to love it. The same applies to food choices. In that aspect food likes and dislikes work exactly the same as your taste in music – it comes down to exposure and new experiences in comparison to past experiences. The food you grew up hating can now become the food you grow to love …

Spinach

I am most certainly not the only person who, while growing up, disliked green vegetables in any shape, size or form. And yet, isn't it funny how leafy greens have suddenly become so trendy! For me, spinach was a big no-no – everyone knew to never bring morogo near me! But one day Thuli, my eldest sister (who avoids setting foot in a kitchen as far as possible because she still remembers all those tinned-fish sandwiches much too vividly), surprised us with a new dish that completely bowled us over and changed my mind about spinach forever. So here is Thuli's utterly delicious recipe – it's just too good not to share with you. And the best part? It is extremely easy to make!

Spinach with Chorizo Sausage

Great as an accompaniment or as a main meal with a starch of your choice. The secret ingredient that adds the magic to this dish, is the almond flakes!

Serves 4

45 ml vegetable oil
1 medium tomato, peeled and diced
10 ml Wet Masala Paste Mix (see page 36)
salt and pepper, to taste
1–2 chorizo, sliced (± 225 g)
100 ml plain yoghurt
more oil, for frying
400 g baby spinach
50 g almond flakes, toasted

1. Heat the oil in a skillet over moderate heat.
2. Add the tomatoes, masala, salt and pepper, and stir through.
3. Add the sausage slices and stir through.
4. Add the yoghurt and stir through.
5. Simmer over low heat for 10 minutes or until cooked through.
6. In a separate pan, heat some more oil and pan-fry the spinach for 3 minutes.
7. Remove from the stove and let it stand for 10 minutes before you dish up.
8. To serve, first layer the cooked spinach on a wooden board or platter, then add the sausage slices and garnish with the almond flakes or any nuts of your choice.

Steamed Spinach Bread
(Ujeqe)

Now that I have warmed up to spinach, I find that it actually adds depth to the flavour of a whole range of dishes. This recipe has its origin in the fact that I wanted to add an interesting twist to our conventional steamed bread. It proved to be such a hit, not only with my friends but also on social media, that some people now consider this recipe "a national treasure" – I loved this response!

Makes 1 medium loaf to serve 4

360 g (3 cups / 750 ml) flour
10 g (1 sachet) dry yeast
a pinch of salt
a pinch of sugar
125 ml warm water
125 ml warm milk
1 large egg
30 ml vegetable oil
500 g chopped baby spinach

1. Mix all the dry ingredients first, then add the wet ingredients to form a dough.
2. You may knead the dough with your hands, but I prefer to use an electric mixer.
3. When all the ingredients are combined thoroughly, transfer the dough onto a dry surface and knead it into a small ball shape. The dough will be sticky.
4. Place the dough in a large, greased bowl and cover with cling wrap. Let it stand in a warm place to rise for 30 minutes or until it has tripled in volume.
5. Oil a medium-sized metal bowl.
6. In a large pot, boil 1 litre of water. Knock the dough down and place it in the metal bowl over the pot.
7. Cover with the pot's lid, and cook over low heat for 1 hour or until a knife comes out clean when inserted into the centre of the bread.
8. Serve with any protein of your choice – I love it with oxtail (see Oxtail Stew in Red Wine on page 127).

Pumpkin

Any pumpkin, including butternut, was never something I took a liking to until I tasted this dish created by my friend Nwabisa Mabandla. Now it has become one of my firm favourites because it oozes warm-heartedness. It never fails to create new memories as sweet as the dish itself, even though I do not add a single granule of sugar. The cinnamon and vanilla do the trick effortlessly in any kind of pumpkin dish. It is quite a hit at home in Umlazi, especially over Christmas.

Butternut Pie

Serves 6

butter, to grease
flour, to dust
500 g butternut, oven-roasted with cinnamon
250 ml White Star Super Maize Meal
2 medium eggs
150 g butter
150 ml fresh cream
10 ml vanilla extract
200 ml flour, sifted
2.5 ml baking powder

1. Preheat the oven to 180 °C.
2. Grease an ovenproof pie dish with a little butter and then dust with flour.
3. Place the rest of the ingredients in the large bowl of an electric mixer and mix at medium speed for 6 to 8 minutes.
4. Once the mixture has a smooth texture, transfer it to the pie dish and bake for 45 minutes, or until golden on top.
5. Serve as a side or an accompaniment to any protein.

Potatoes

Ever since I was a kid, I hated potatoes passionately. I think it is the mushiness that puts me off. No-one could ever convince me to eat mashed potatoes. Thuli always teases me and says, "So how come you can have fish and chips then?" Well, my answer is simple: When the chips are crispy, they don't taste like potatoes.

A nice nutritional fact: the healthiest part of a potato is its skin – it is packed with vitamins, iron and potassium. Fortunately, I love potato skins!

This recipe is ideal if you want to treat people to something out of the ordinary or when you are having friends over to watch the soccer and you want to impress them with a snack other than the usual.

Loaded Bacon and Potato Skins

Serves 4

8 medium potatoes, washed
30 ml vegetable oil
sea salt and black pepper
extra oil, for frying
200 g streaky bacon
250 g plain cottage cheese
30 ml lemon juice
2 spring onions, chopped

1. Preheat the oven to 180 °C.
2. Peel the potatoes and make sure that there is enough flesh left on the skins for texture.
3. Pour the oil onto a baking tray.
4. Season the oil with salt and pepper.
5. Toss the potato skins in the oil and then oven-roast them for 15 minutes or until crispy.
6. In a medium-sized pan, heat a little oil and fry the bacon until crispy. Break or cut it into pieces.
7. Set aside on paper towel.
8. Transfer the cottage cheese into a small bowl, season with salt and pepper, add the lemon juice and mix well.
9. On a medium-sized plate or platter, arrange the potato skins and then the bacon pieces.
10. Add dollops of cottage cheese and sprinkle with spring onions.

Cabbage

Growing up, I used to hate the smell of cabbage cooking and I never understood why anyone would willingly make or enjoy a cabbage or potato curry. I firmly believe cabbage and potatoes should be reserved as side dishes, but during my childhood both of these used to make their frequent appearance as weekday main meals.

But I have come a long way and nowadays I like experimenting with ingredients I never liked. One of my more successful attempts resulted in this new take on traditional coleslaw.

Coleslaw

This coleslaw has a colourful twist – I replace the traditional white cabbage with red cabbage to give it an edge, and I add apple for a yummy crunch. A great salad for a braai, or the ideal filling for a fresh sandwich. The dash of lime juice adds a bit of tanginess, and prevents the apple from turning brown.

Serves 4

250 g shredded red cabbage
5 ml sesame oil
1 green pepper, deseeded and cut into strips
1 yellow pepper, deseeded and cut into strips
1 red pepper, deseeded and cut into strips
1 medium red apple, cut into thin strips or grated
4 spring onions, chopped
80 ml chopped fresh coriander
a pinch of white sugar
45 ml pineapple juice
a dash of lime

1. In a medium-sized bowl, mix all the ingredients together.
2. Set aside or refrigerate until needed.

Tips

- Coleslaw can last in the fridge for up to a week.
- This coleslaw can be served with any kind of braai meat.
- At home, we always enjoy this refreshing salad with everyday meals.

Samp

Sometimes something unexpected happens and it scars your opinion of certain foods. This is what happened to me and samp. It was back in the 1980s. Unexpectedly, Mom comes home with a brand new TV. We were one of the first houses in Umlazi to have one – it was such a treat! One of my sisters was cooking supper that night, and she decided on samp and beans. In the commotion of getting the TV set up and with all the excitement, she forgot to check the pot and she burnt the samp. My Mom was fuming, and as punishment she insisted we eat the samp. The end result? We all had the worst stomach ache, and from that day on I could never again stand the smell or taste of samp. That was the case, until my younger brother Sandile's wife, Thandeka, introduced me to her samp dish …

What makes Thandeka's recipe so special is that she fries it just like you would cook fried rice. For me, this was the culinary game-changer when it comes to samp.

Another important element is the beans. I know there are many different ways of cooking samp in South Africa, but personally I find a samp dish incomplete without the beans.

Samp and Beans

Serves 6

500 g samp, soaked in water
500 g beans of your choice, soaked in water
4 litres of water
a pinch of salt
20 ml vegetable oil
1 medium onion, finely chopped
salt and pepper, to taste
5 ml chopped fresh garlic and ginger
5 ml mild masala curry powder
2 medium tomatoes, peeled and finely chopped

Optional
Meaty bones, chicken, beef or mixed veggies of your choice

1. Rinse the samp and beans to remove the starchy water.
2. Transfer the samp and beans into a large pot and fill with water.
3. Add a pinch of salt, stir through, and then cook over low heat for 2 hours or until soft. (I usually cook mine in a slow cooker overnight.)
4. When the samp and beans are cooked, set aside.
5. In a large pan, heat the vegetable oil for a minute.
6. Add the onion and cook until translucent.
7. Add the salt and pepper, garlic and ginger, and masala. Stir through.
8. Add the tomatoes, stir and cook for about a minute.
9. Add the meaty bones, chicken, beef or mixed vegetables, if using. Cook for 2 minutes, or if using bones, chicken or beef, make sure that it is cooked through.
10. Now add the samp and beans gradually in batches. Make sure that it soaks up all the sauce.

Chicken

When I was younger, I loathed Zulu chicken, or hard-body chicken, as it is fondly called by most folks. The Xhosa people call it umleqwa.

I hated the smell of it. So once again my sister-in-law Thandeka introduced me to a recipe that has irrevocably changed my mind. Not only does it taste delicious, but the flavour also intensifies and the next day the leftover chicken is even tastier served cold.

It is a very simple recipe with only a few easy steps to follow, and with very few ingredients.

Zulu Chicken

Umleqwa *or hand-raised Zulu chicken is sold at most supermarkets or local meat markets. Replace it with an ordinary whole chicken if you have difficulty sourcing a hard body.*

Serves 6

1 large whole chicken
500 ml cold water
10 ml sea salt
2 cubes of store-bought chicken stock
1 medium onion, roughly chopped
4 medium spring onions, finely chopped

1. If using proper hard-body chicken, clean the bird carefully and properly before cooking.
2. Pour the cold water into a large pot, add the salt and stock, and stir until dissolved.
3. Put the whole chicken in the seasoned water while it is still heating up, put the lid on the pot, and cook over low heat for ± 1½ hours or until tender.
4. Add all of the onions during the last 5 minutes of the cooking time so that the onion flavour is not overpowering.
5. Serve with *pap* or Steamed Spinach Bread (*ujeqe*) (see page 44).

Prawns

To be honest, I never thought that I could and would eat prawns. The first time I ever laid my eyes on these crustaceans, I only saw creepy crawlies that looked scary and inedible. But when I was served my first prawn cocktail, I changed my mind – it looked so elegant in the tall glass. It was garnished with thin slices of mango, which made it difficult for me to resist. And that is how I started liking and enjoying prawns. I went on to experiment with preparing them in all kinds of ways: grilled in garlic, prawn curry in yoghurt and cream, or prawn and chicken curry … Here is my own take on a prawn cocktail, and even if I say so myself, this is a truly delectable dish.

Prawn Cocktail

Serves 4

15 g (15 ml) butter
400 g prawns, peeled and pre-cooked
10 ml chilli flakes
salt and pepper, to taste
1 whole mango, peeled and cubed (if it is not in season, replace with melon or papaya)
150 ml mayonnaise
10 ml Masala Mix, wet or dry (see page 36)
2.5 ml turmeric
80 g chopped rocket, chopped Italian parsley and edible flowers, to garnish

1. Heat the butter in a skillet over moderate to high heat.
2. Dust the prawns with chilli flakes, salt and pepper.
3. Sauté the prawns on each side for about 2 minutes.
4. Transfer the cooked prawns into a bowl lined with paper towel.
5. Set aside to cool.
6. Mix the mayo and masala to make a currynaise sauce.
7. First put some mango cubes in the bottom of 4 clear, tall wine glasses.
8. Add a bit of currynaise on top of the mango.
9. Place the prawns on top of the sauce and garnish with rocket, Italian parsley and edible flowers.

Trifle

Traditional trifle is a dessert that I totally loathed as a child – I think I was completely put off by the sponge cake soaked in all that liquid which made it so dreadfully soggy. Here is my preferred, more elegant alternative to trifle. Instead of a large bowl of clashing colours that kind of resembles a carefully constructed layered dessert, mine really is a carefully constructed layered dessert.

Trifle á la Lucia

You need to take into account that the first layer is actually a panna cotta and it must be refrigerated over night, so start preparing this dessert a day in advance.

Serves 6

Layer 1
150 ml milk
40 ml gelatine powder
650 ml fresh cream
125 g (155 ml) white sugar
15 ml vanilla extract

Layer 2
250 ml boiling water
3 x 40 g strawberry jelly powder
125 ml cold water
125 g strawberries, sliced
80 g blackberries, if in season
80 g raspberries or blueberries
500 ml fresh cream, whipped
125 ml coconut flakes, toasted

DAY 1 – For the panna cotta layer:
1. Pour the milk into a bowl, add the gelatine and set aside.
2. In a saucepan, mix the cream with the sugar and cook over low heat. Allow to boil, but be careful not to let it boil over.
3. Pour the milk mixture into the cream while stirring continuously until it is completely dissolved.
4. Add the vanilla to the mixture and stir through.
5. Pour the mixture into a trifle dish or divide it evenly into 6 medium wine glasses.
6. Refrigerate overnight.

DAY 2 – For the strawberry jelly layer:
1. Pour the boiling water into a medium-sized bowl.
2. Add the strawberry jelly powder.
3. Add the cold water and mix until completely dissolved.
4. Set aside to cool.
5. Once completely cooled down, pour the liquid into the trifle dish with the panna cotta layer, which should now be firmly set. Let this jelly layer set by putting the trifle back in the fridge for ± 45 minutes.
6. Once set, layer with berries and top with whipped cream.
7. Sprinkle with coconut flakes.
8. Serve chilled.

Seven Colours

Seven Colours is a traditional South African meal that would include chicken or beef, rice and a variety of colourful side dishes: pumpkin, sweet potato, beetroot, cabbage, green beans or a bean salad, potato salad, coleslaw ... and to add the final touch that binds together the whole array of colour: trifle for pudding!

In the township where I grew up in Umlazi, we kept the tradition of having a seven-colour Sunday lunch and we looked forward to this treat the whole week. Come Sunday morning bright and early, we would wake up, get up and dress in our Sunday best, and walk to our church, the Uganda Parish. The service lasted for about an hour and a half, and the highlight for me was singing in the choir as well as performing as a soloist.

My favourite day was filled with my favourite things: food and music. It energised me and filled me with a joy that would spill over into the rest of the week. It would last me the next six days until the seventh day would again be filled with seven colours and soulful singing.

Most weeks we were lucky enough to have leftovers from Sunday lunch that would make its way into Monday's lunchboxes to brighten our day when we lifted the lid.

Today, Sunday still is a very special day that I choose to spend with family and friends. When I am not cooking one of my speciality curry dishes, I still fill my Sundays with seven colours and some singing. And, as with most traditions, it is always best shared with family and friends.

Beetroot Salad

Beetroot is the one salad that will never fail to make its appearance at a seven-colour Sunday lunch right across South Africa. I'd even be so bold as to say that beetroot salad has become quite a bore. So, I have started adding other elements, like sweet pineapple, to give it a refreshing new flavour.

Serves 4

4 medium beetroots
1 medium red onion, thinly sliced
15 ml extra-virgin olive oil
60 ml red wine vinegar
250 ml fresh pineapple cubes OR 1 x 440 g can pineapple pieces
125 g plain feta cheese, cubed
6 spring onions, sliced

1. Boil the beetroot in water for 20-25 minutes or until soft. Set aside to cool.
2. Once cooled, peel them and then slice thinly into a salad bowl.
3. Add the onion rings.
4. In a separate small bowl, mix the oil and vinegar thoroughly and drizzle over the beets and onion.
5. Toss so that the beetroot and onion are covered all over with the dressing.
6. Add the pineapple and feta cheese on top. Do not mix.
7. Garnish with spring onions and serve cold.

Remember

Beetroot will make anything you add to it change colour if it is left in the beetroot juice for too long, so add the other elements just before serving.

Grilled Butternut

Serves 4

500 g peeled and cubed butternut OR 2 small whole butternuts
30 ml honey
30 ml olive oil
5 ml ground cinnamon

1. Preheat the oven to 180 °C.
2. If using a whole butternut, cut it in half, scoop out the pips and cut into 6 to 8 wedges.
3. Spread the butternut out on a baking tray.
4. Drizzle with honey and olive oil, and generously sprinkle with cinnamon. Toss well to coat all over.
5. Bake for 30 minutes or until golden.

White Cabbage

When I grew up, cabbage used to be a plain side dish. It was cooked by just boiling it in salted water. I came up with a far more exciting way to enjoy cabbage, and it's delicious!

Serves 6

45 ml vegetable oil
1 medium white onion, finely chopped
5 ml honey
15 ml medium masala
15 ml crushed garlic and ginger paste
½ white cabbage, shredded
salt and pepper, to taste

1. In a medium saucepan, heat the oil and add the onion. Sauté for 1 minute.
2. Add the honey, masala, garlic and ginger, and stir through.
3. Add the cabbage and mix well.
4. Season with salt and pepper.
5. Serve hot or cold.

Green Beans

This recipe is for a warm green bean dish, but the dish can also be served cold.

Serves 6

30 g butter
15 ml crushed garlic
15 ml dry chilli flakes
400 g green beans, ends trimmed
salt and pepper, to taste
15 ml lemon zest

1. Heat the butter in a medium-sized saucepan.
2. Add the garlic and chilli. Fry for 1 minute. Set aside.
3. In a medium pot, bring salted water to the boil. Blanche the green beans for 2 to 3 minutes in the water until crisp. Drain and transfer into the saucepan with the melted butter. Toss to coat.
4. Season with salt and pepper.
5. Transfer to a serving dish.
6. Sprinkle with lemon zest.

For a cold green bean dish:
1. First blanche the green beans, drain and then cover with cold water and ice cubes to stop the cooking process and keep them bright green.
2. Heat the butter in a small pan.
3. Add the garlic and chilli. Fry for 1 minute.
4. Drain the green beans and transfer onto a serving plate.
5. Drizzle with the melted butter.
6. Season with salt and pepper.
7. Garnish with lemon zest.

Roast Beef Fillet

Beef was never my favourite meat, until I tasted beef fillet. Once again, thanks to my friend Nicola, now a prominent chef in Europe. We used to share an apartment in Bryanston and he loved cooking steak, but he'd never share. I, on the other hand, was taught that food is for sharing. But one day I saw how expensive this cut of meat actually was. I bought it out of curiosity and prepared it medium – the first bite was pure bliss.

Serves 4–6

1.5 kg beef fillet
30 ml olive oil
15 ml coarse sea salt
10 ml freshly ground black pepper
8 sprigs of rosemary
8 sprigs of thyme
12 cloves of garlic, sliced

1. Heat a medium skillet or large pan.
2. Preheat the oven to 180 °C.
3. If preferred, butterfly the fillet (otherwise keep it whole).
4. Rub the meat with the oil, salt and pepper.
5. Brown the meat for 5 minutes on each side in the piping hot pan.
6. Cover the pan with foil.
7. Reduce the oven temperature to 160 °C and roast the meat for 1½ hours.
8. Once cooked, remove the foil and sprinkle the rosemary, thyme and garlic over the steak.
9. Again cover with foil and let it rest for 15 to 20 minutes, depending on how you like your meat done, before serving.

Serving suggestion

Fillet steak is very filling. While everyone knows the steak-and-chips combination, most people prefer to rather have a light, refreshing side, like a salad in summer or roasted veg in winter (see Oven-Roasted Vegetables, page 72). But why not try something new like my Sweet Potato Fries (see page 124) – they're a winner!

Fried Turmeric Rice

Fried rice is one of my favourite dishes because of all the colour you can incorporate into it. Visually it is a feast for the eyes and contributes to the Seven Colours theme. I add the asparagus and mushrooms, and I also prefer frying the eggs separately and adding the scramble as a garnish instead of mixing it into the rice.

Serves 5

500 ml rice of your choice (I prefer basmati)
750 ml chicken stock
5 ml turmeric OR egg yolk powder (available at Indian spice shops)
a pinch of salt
60 g butter
50 ml vegetable oil
1 onion, thinly sliced
5 ml fresh ginger and garlic paste
5 ml leaf masala
500 g mixed fresh vegetables, diced, e.g. red, yellow and green pepper, blanched asparagus, carrots and green beans)
125 g mushrooms, sliced
1 bay leaf
2 eggs
50 ml milk
salt and pepper, to taste
30 ml chopped fresh coriander, to garnish

1. In a medium bowl, soak the rice in water for 15 minutes.
2. Drain the rice and transfer into a large saucepan with a lid.
3. Add the stock, turmeric and salt, and stir through.
4. Bring the rice to a boil over high heat.
5. Once it starts boiling, reduce the heat and cook covered for about 5 minutes – remember you still have to fry it, so do not overcook it at this stage.
6. Fluff the rice with a fork to separate the grains, then set aside.
7. Heat the butter and the oil in a large saucepan.
8. Add the onion and sauté until translucent.
9. Add the garlic and ginger paste and masala, and stir through.
10. Add all the vegetables, except the mushrooms.
11. Cook over high heat for about 5 minutes.
12. Add the mushrooms and bay leaf. Stir through.
13. Stir in the half-cooked rice, then cover the saucepan with a lid and let it steam for about 10 minutes.
14. In a medium bowl, beat the eggs, milk and salt and pepper together, and then scramble in a medium pan for about 1 minute – keep whisking the mix until cooked.
15. Garnish the rice with the scrambled eggs and coriander.

Oven-Roasted Vegetables

Vegetables bring vibrancy to the lunch table and without a mixed veg dish, the Seven Colours would be incomplete.

Serves 6

1 large butternut, peeled and cut into chunks
3 large potatoes, cut into chunks
1 medium red onion, cut into small chunks
3 robot peppers (1 yellow pepper, 1 red pepper, 1 green pepper), deseeded and cut into 3-cm squares
1 bulb garlic, cloves separated and peeled OR 1 bulb halved horizontally
sea salt and freshly ground black pepper
1 bunch of medium-sized beetroot, beets halved or cut into chunks
30 ml extra-virgin olive oil, for drizzling

1. Place 2 baking trays in the oven and preheat to 230 °C.
2. In a large bowl, combine the butternut, potatoes, onion, peppers and garlic. Drizzle with olive oil, season with salt and pepper, and toss to coat everything all over with oil.
3. In a separate bowl, drizzle the beet chunks with olive oil and toss to coat all over.
4. Transfer onto the baking trays and roast for about 45 minutes at 180 °C.
5. If you halved the garlic bulb horizontally, squeeze some of the garlic cloves out of their skins after roasting and toss through the rest of the roasted vegetables.

Rainbow Trifle

Trifle is the epitome of Seven Colours, because of the vibrancy of the layers. There's no wrong or right way when it comes to trifle. Most people prefer to use a large glass bowl so that the layers are clearly visible. I like making individual trifles in glasses and adding fresh fruit instead of stewed or canned fruit.

Serves 6

80 g red jelly powder
80 g green jelly powder
480 ml hot water
480 ml cold water
1 quantity Home-Made Custard (see page 160)
250 g strawberries, sliced if necessary (reserve some for garnishing)
100 g blackberries
100 g raspberries
250 ml fresh cream
10 ml castor sugar
a sprig of mint

1. Place the red jelly powder in a large clear bowl, and place the green jelly powder in another large bowl.
2. Add 240 ml hot water to each bowl, and stir through.
3. Add 240 ml cold water to each bowl, and stir through.
4. Refrigerate until the jelly is set.
5. Make the custard and leave it to cool.
6. Use 6 separate glasses, and start layering the trifle with spoonfuls of jelly as the bottom layer. Alternatively, take the bowl of red jelly as your trifle bowl, and spoon the green jelly into a layer on top of the red jelly.
7. Then add a layer of strawberries, followed by a layer of custard.
8. Then add a layer of blackberries, followed by a layer of custard.
9. Then add a layer of raspberries, followed by a layer of custard.
10. If there are jelly, berries and custard left, continue layering. Remember to reserve some of the strawberries for garnishing.
11. Whip the fresh cream while adding the castor sugar to it. Keep on whisking until it forms stiff peaks.
12. Finish the trifle with a top layer of whipped cream.
13. Garnish with mint leaves and the remaining strawberries.

Curry Queen

Among family, friends, fans and followers, I have become known not only as the Kitchen Queen, but as their Curry Queen as well. It all started when I decided to experiment with various ingredients like butter, amasi (sour cream), yoghurt and fresh cream. Now I cannot imagine cooking without these ingredients.

I usually cook curries on Sundays, and let me tell you: I get a lot of calls from family and friends asking me if they are invited for lunch! As a result, I have stopped posting any of my "Curry Sunday" pics on social media, because I always end up having a full house by lunch time and come Sunday night I am left with a house full of dirty dishes.

My curries can be best described as a cross between North and South Indian styles. Don't ask me how I came up with adding and combining the different ingredients that I now trust to transform my curries – it was a process of trial and error until I realised I had struck gold. After receiving requests to share my curry secrets, I started to focus some of my cooking classes on teaching others my curry tricks. These classes are always fully booked way in advance.

For me there is one basic way of cooking the perfect curry. From there on I only adjust the cooking time depending on what kind of curry I am cooking. And one golden tip: always keep a kettle of boiling water handy when you cook curry because when spices stick to the bottom of your pot or pan, you need to quickly loosen them with a dash of boiling water without altering the consistency of your curry sauce.

Here are my most foolproof curry recipes …

Yoghurt and Cream Lamb Curry

This is my signature dish and a golden go-to curry recipe. One of my followers on social media even called it a national treasure. I use plain yoghurt or amasi *(sour milk) to make it rich and flavourful. It is also very important to use a good masala (see my Wet or Dry Masala Mix recipes on page 36). And remember to keep the kettle of boiling water handy!*

Serves 4

- 200 ml plain yoghurt
- 500 g lamb knuckles
- 30 g butter
- 30 ml vegetable oil
- 1 onion, finely chopped
- 2 cloves garlic, crushed
- 10 ml ginger
- 15 ml chopped curry leaves
- 30 ml leaf masala or Wet Masala Paste Mix (see page 36)
- salt and pepper, to taste
- 150 ml boiling water
- 1 tomato, peeled and finely chopped
- 10 ml tomato paste
- 200 ml fresh cream
- 30 ml chopped fresh coriander
- cooked rice or roti

1. In a bowl, pour the yoghurt over the lamb knuckles and let it marinade for at least 10 hours, but preferably overnight.
2. Heat the butter and oil in a heavy skillet that has a lid.
3. Add the onion, garlic, ginger, curry leaves, masala, and salt and pepper.
4. Stir through and sauté for about 5 minutes until the onion is golden brown.
5. Add the marinated lamb knuckles and stir through thoroughly.
6. Lower the heat, add the boiling water, stir through and cover with the lid.
7. Let it cook for 1 hour and only lift the lid when stirring from time to time.
8. When cooked thoroughly, add the tomato and tomato paste, and stir through.
9. Again cover with the lid and let the curry simmer for another 15 minutes.
10. Add the fresh cream and stir through.
11. Simmer for 5 minutes.
12. Garnish with the coriander, and serve the curry with rice or roti.

Chicken Curry

Again, the secret to a good curry is the masala or curry powder you choose to use, and to marinate the meat overnight in yoghurt or amasi. *I prefer deboned chicken thighs. It is important to cut the chicken into smaller, evenly sized pieces so that it cooks evenly. If you use whole chicken pieces, remember that it will increase the cooking time.*

Serves 6

500 g chicken thigh fillets
200 ml plain yoghurt
30 g butter
15 ml vegetable oil
1 onion, finely chopped
30 ml mild curry powder
1 green chilli, finely chopped (optional)
10 ml crushed garlic
5 ml ginger
5 ml salt
freshly ground black pepper, to taste
100 ml boiling water
1 tomato, finely chopped
200 ml fresh cream
30 ml chopped fresh coriander, to garnish
cooked rice or roti, to serve

1. Cut the meat into smaller, evenly sized pieces, add the yoghurt and let it marinade for at least for 10 hours, but preferably overnight.
2. Heat the butter and oil in a heavy skillet that has a lid.
3. Add the onion, curry powder, chilli (if using), garlic, ginger, salt and pepper.
4. Stir through and cook the onion until translucent.
5. Add the marinated meat and stir through thoroughly.
6. Keep the boiling water close by and add a little to the mix the moment it looks like the meat is sticking to the bottom of the skillet.
7. Cover with the lid and turn down the heat.
8. Cook for 10 minutes and only lift the lid while stirring.
9. When cooked thoroughly, add the tomato and stir through.
10. Cover with the lid and let the curry simmer for another 10 minutes.
11. Add the fresh cream and stir through.
12. Simmer for a further 5 minutes.
13. Garnish with the coriander, and serve the curry with rice or roti.

Beef Curry with Jasmine Rice

A lunch buffet is not complete without beef curry. I like to use beef fillet or rump steak, because these cuts are the most tender. If you cook this curry the night before, it will taste even better the next day because by then the flavours of all the spices would have had time to develop.

Serves 4

30 ml butter
30 ml vegetable oil
1 medium onion, chopped
15 ml crushed garlic
15 ml minced ginger
salt and pepper, to taste
15 ml Wet or Dry Masala Mix (see page 36)
1 x 410 g can chopped tomatoes
15 ml tomato paste
1 kg beef (rump or fillet), cubed
30 ml chopped fresh coriander
cooked basmati rice or Jasmine Rice (recipe below), to serve

1. Heat a heavy skillet, and melt the butter and oil together.
2. Add the onion, garlic, ginger, salt and pepper, as well as the masala mix. Sauté until the onion is golden brown.
3. Add the tomatoes and tomato paste, and mix to combine.
4. Add the meat and stir through.
5. Prevent the curry from burning by adding a little boiling water to the mix, if necessary.
6. Cover the skillet and turn down the heat. Simmer for 30 minutes while keeping the lid on. Open only when you need to stir it.
7. Garnish with coriander.
8. Serve with basmati rice or Jasmine Rice.

Jasmine Rice

30 g butter
1 onion, chopped
2 bay leaves
2.5 ml ginger
2.5 ml crushed garlic
5 ml turmeric
500 ml jasmine rice
1 stock cube
750 ml water
fresh coriander, to garnish

1. In a wok or deep enough skillet, heat the butter and sauté the onion until golden.
2. Add the bay leaves, ginger and garlic. Fry for 2 minutes.
3. Add the turmeric, and stir through.
4. Add the rice and keep on stirring for about 2 minutes.
5. Add the stock cube and water, and bring to the boil.
6. Cover and let it simmer over low heat for 15 minutes.
7. Remove from the heat and let it stand for 10 minutes.
8. Fluff the rice with a fork to separate the grains.
9. Garnish with coriander.

Prawn Curry

I never liked prawns until a friend very convincingly changed my mind. You just need to prepare the prawns properly to be able to appreciate them. This recipe can also be used to make a quick chicken curry (different from the Chicken Curry on page 80 in that the chicken is not marinated), but be sure to use deboned skinless chicken thighs cut into smaller, evenly sized pieces.

Serves 6

10 ml vegetable oil
30 g butter
1 medium onion, chopped
10 ml garlic and ginger
a pinch of salt and pepper
5 ml medium Wet Masala Paste Mix (see page 36)
5–10 ml dry red chilli flakes OR 1–2 red chillies, finely chopped
10 ml tomato paste
400 g peeled prawns
200 ml coconut cream
15 ml chopped fresh coriander
juice of 1 fresh lime
cooked poppadoms, to serve

1. In a shallow pan, heat the oil and butter together.
2. Add the onion and fry until golden.
3. Add the garlic and ginger, and stir through.
4. Add the salt and pepper, masala and chilli, and stir through.
5. Add the tomato paste, mix well and cook over low heat for about 3 minutes.
6. Add the prawns and cook for 2 minutes on each side.
7. Add the coconut cream, and gently stir through to combine.
8. Let it simmer for about 5 minutes.
9. Garnish with coriander.
10. Squeeze the lime juice over the dish.
11. Serve with poppadoms.

Mince Curry

This quick and easy dish is a firm favourite in most South African homes, especially as a weekday meal. You can substitute beef mince with turkey or chicken mince – all variations are delicious.

Serves 4

30 ml vegetable oil
10 g butter
1 medium onion, finely chopped
2 cloves garlic, crushed
5 ml minced fresh ginger
15 ml Dry Masala Powder Mix (see page 36)
5 ml paprika
1 sprig curry leaves, chopped OR 15 dry curry leaves
1 red chilli, minced
500 g beef mince
1 medium tomato, peeled and finely chopped
10 ml tomato paste
salt and pepper
200 g butternut, oven-roasted and drizzled with honey
chopped fresh coriander, to garnish
rice, vetkoek or roti, to serve

1. Heat the oil and butter in a hot pan.
2. Add the onion, garlic and ginger and fry until soft and translucent.
3. Add the masala, paprika, curry leaves and chilli, and stir through.
4. Add the mince and stir with a fork until all the lumps are loosened. Add a little water if necessary.
5. Add the tomato and let it simmer covered for about 10 minutes.
6. Add the tomato paste and season with salt and pepper.
7. Add the butternut and check the seasoning.
8. Garnish with coriander.
9. Serve on rice, or in vetkoek or roti.

Three-Bean Curry

I always take a break from meat when I want to lose weight. This three bean curry is wholesome and truly delicious. Steamed bread and beans was my late mother's favourite dish. The simplicity of her recipe is something to marvel at – you can easily prepare it any day of the week as a dinner treat. I have given it my own twist by adding two more types of beans. Use canned beans to save you even more time!

Serves 6

30 ml vegetable oil
1 medium onion, finely chopped
10 ml chopped garlic
10 ml minced ginger
salt and pepper, to taste
5 ml ground cumin
5 ml ground coriander
1 x 410 g can chopped tomatoes
10 g tomato paste
5 ml smoked paprika
5 ml turmeric
200 ml coconut cream
1 x 410 g can kidney beans, drained and rinsed
1 x 400 g can black beans, drained and rinsed
1 x 400 g can chickpeas, drained and rinsed
15 ml chopped fresh parsley
cooked basmati rice or flatbread, to serve

1. Heat the oil in a heavy skillet.
2. Add the onion, garlic and ginger, and cook while stirring for 5 minutes.
3. Add salt and pepper and stir through.
4. In a separate pan, roast the cumin and coriander for about 2 minutes until brown. Then add it to the cooked onion mix. Stir through.
5. Add the tomatoes, tomato paste, paprika and turmeric, and stir through well.
6. Add the coconut cream, stir through and lower the temperature to simmering heat.
7. Add all three cans of beans. Let it simmer for about 5 minutes.
8. Garnish with coriander.
9. Serve with basmati rice or flatbread.

Meatballs in a Curry Sauce

This is a great weeknight supper! Serve with rice.

Serves 4

Meatballs

500 g beef mince
1 medium egg
1 medium onion, finely chopped
125 ml finely chopped mixed peppers
10 ml crushed garlic
10 ml minced ginger
15 ml chopped fresh thyme
125 ml fresh breadcrumbs
salt and pepper, to taste
60 ml vegetable oil

1. Mix together the beef, egg, onion, peppers, garlic, ginger, thyme, breadcrumbs, salt and pepper.
2. Use the mixture to shape golf ball-sized meatballs.
3. Heat the oil in a non-stick frying pan. Fry the meatballs in it, shaking the pan often.
4. Once cooked, transfer onto paper towel to drain any excess oil.

Curry Sauce

50 ml vegetable oil
50 g butter or ghee
1 medium onion, finely chopped
10 ml ground cumin
10 ml ground coriander
salt and pepper
20 ml leaf masala powder
1 medium-sized ripe tomato, peeled and chopped
10 ml tomato paste
150 ml coconut cream

To serve
cooked rice or Steamed Spinach Bread (see page 44)
20 ml chopped fresh coriander, to garnish

1. Heat the oil and butter in a saucepan.
2. Add the onion and sauté.
3. Add the cumin and coriander, salt and pepper, and stir through.
4. Add the masala and cook for 2 minutes. Add a splash of boiling water if the mixture starts to stick to the bottom of the saucepan.
5. Add the tomato, tomato paste and coconut cream. Stir through.
6. Cook over low heat for 3 minutes.
7. Then let it simmer for another minute to thicken, and set aside.
8. Place the meatballs in the curry sauce.

To serve:
- Serve the meatballs in the curry sauce on rice or with steamed bread to soak up all the delicious sauce.
- Garnish with coriander.

Tamarind Fish Curry

I was visiting my aunt in Pietermaritzburg when I tasted fish curry for the first time. I have so many wonderful memories of my aunt's house – she really knew her way around the kitchen. While I was spending my summer holiday with her, she made a fresh fish curry for dinner one evening. It tasted rather good, but it did not agree with me at all. During the night I got really sick, and it took me probably the next 20 years to convince myself to try a fresh fish curry again. My niece Nothile shared her delicious recipe with me, and now, thanks to her, this tamarind fish curry is my favourite.

Serves 4–6

60 ml canola oil
1 large onion, chopped
15 ml crushed garlic
30 ml medium leaf masala powder
1 x 410 g can chopped tomatoes
250 ml plain yoghurt
30 ml tomato sauce
60 ml tomato paste
15 ml tamarind
salt and pepper

1 kg firm fish steaks (like tilapia or Cape salmon)
30 g (60 ml) flour, for dusting
juice of 1 medium lemon
30 ml chopped fresh coriander, to serve

cooked basmati rice or roti, to serve

1. Heat half of the oil in a medium-sized pot, add the onion and the garlic. Fry for about 3 minutes or until the onion is translucent.
2. Add the masala and stir through.
3. Add the tomatoes and yoghurt. Stir through.
4. Add the tomato sauce, tomato paste and tamarind. Mix well.
5. Season with salt and pepper.
6. Cook over low heat, covered, for about 5 minutes.

Pre-cooking fish

1. Heat a pan and add the rest of the oil.
2. In a medium bowl, dust the fish fillets with flour and fry them for 2 minutes on each side.
3. Once cooked, set them aside on paper towel.
4. Add the cooked fish to the cooked tomato and onion mix.
5. Let it rest in the mixture for about 2 minutes, then scoop the mix up and pour over the fish fillets. Make sure the fish is covered in the sauce all over.
6. Cook over low heat for 10 minutes.
7. Garnish with coriander.
8. Serve with basmati rice or roti.

Butter Chicken a.k.a. Murgh Makhani

I remember when I moved into my new place in Bryanston, I came across an old recipe book that people who had stayed there before me, had left behind. I opened the book and found a hand-written note that said, "Check page 160 – this dish is delicious!" I could not wait to try out the recipe, and ever since then this has become my go-to recipe for special occasions.

Serves 6

Marinade
15 ml crushed garlic and ginger mix
15 ml garam masala
5 ml ground coriander
5 ml ground cumin
15 ml tomato paste
30 ml lemon juice

Chicken
500 g chicken breast fillets, cut into small pieces

Curry Sauce
60 ml vegetable oil
1 kg ripe tomatoes
120 g butter
salt and freshly ground black pepper, to taste
180 ml fresh cream
1 green chilli, deseeded and julienned
fresh coriander leaves, to garnish
cooked basmati rice, flatbread or roti, to serve
sambals, to serve

1. Mix the garlic and ginger, masala, coriander, cumin and tomato paste with the lemon juice. Rub this mixture into the chicken pieces. Marinade at least for 10 hours, preferably overnight.
2. Brush the grill with some oil to prevent the chicken from sticking. Place the chicken pieces on the grill over extremely hot coals and grill for about 2 minutes on each side. Alternatively, grill the chicken in the oven for 10 minutes.
3. Boil the tomatoes for about 2 minutes, then put them in cold water to cool down. Once cooled, peel and cut into quarters. Remove all the seeds. Then process the remaining tomato flesh in a food processor to a pulp.
4. Place the tomato pulp in a heavy skillet and let it simmer gently until the liquid has evaporated leaving a thick paste. This will take 15 to 20 minutes.
5. Add the butter, salt and pepper. Add the cream and chilli. Stir through thoroughly.
6. Add the chicken pieces and stir through.
7. Simmer gently for about 10 minutes.
8. Transfer the cooked butter chicken into a heated serving dish and garnish with coriander.
9. Serve with rice, flatbread or roti, and sambals on the side.

Maize Starz

Maize is a traditional South African staple and can be used in a wide variety of savoury, side and sweet dishes. I grew up in a home where maize, flour and rice were our three staple ingredients. When I started my cooking classes, I attracted big brands like White Star Super Maize Meal™, who wanted to partner with me if I used maize meal as the main ingredient in approved relevant recipes. I had to come up with various out-of-the-box dishes and I had to develop recipes that would attract followers. In the end I partnered with White Star and a prominent magazine, which advertised my cooking classes and encouraged readers to register for these classes free of charge. This partnership continued successfully for seven years, during which I was tasked to write a booklet consisting of creative recipes for starters, mains, desserts and sides. Here are my most popular maize meal recipes ...

All-Day Breakfast

When you've run out of meal ideas, keep this reliable recipe as ready as a cowboy keeps his gun! If you have leftover pap, this is a great way to make use of it.

Serves 6

240 g (500 ml) maize meal
30 g butter OR 30 ml vegetable oil
½ red onion, thinly sliced
salt and pepper, to taste
a pinch of chilli flakes
500 g pork sausages
250 g butternut cubes, roasted
100 ml chicken or beef stock
125 g cherry tomatoes
1 x 125 g can butter beans, drained
6 medium eggs
25 g Parmesan cheese shavings, to garnish
chopped fresh basil, to garnish

1. Use the maize meal and cook the *pap* as per the instructions for stiff *pap*, as given on the packaging, or use leftover *pap* (see Tips & Tricks with *Pap* below).
2. Lightly grease a rectangular ovenproof dish. Spread the *pap* evenly over the bottom of the dish. Let it set until needed and then cut into 6 squares. (If you do not like squares, roll 12 small *pap* balls and serve 2 per person.)
3. In a large pan, heat the butter or oil.
4. Add the onion, salt, pepper and chilli, and stir for a few seconds or until cooked.
5. Add the sausages and butternut. Cook for about 5 minutes.
6. Stir in the stock to loosen the mix. Keep on stirring occasionally until a golden crust begins to form, then add the cherry tomatoes and beans.
7. Boil or fry the eggs.
8. To assemble, plate each of the six portions by starting with a *pap* square (or 2 *pap* balls), followed by the sausage mix and an egg. Alternatively, you can serve it as in the picture.
9. Garnish with Parmesan and basil.

Tips & Tricks with Pap

Leftover *pap* can be used in so many ways. I always find a way to use *pap* leftovers, whatever the consistency. I usually make my *pap* rather stiff, because it is easy to work with. The recipe above is an excellent example of how to use leftover (*stywe*/stiff) *pap*.

Maize Meal Fish Cakes

An easy weeknight dinner, and the leftovers always work well as part of the next day's lunchbox.

Makes 8 fish cakes

2 potatoes, peeled and cut into small cubes
2 x 170 g cans tuna, drained
2 eggs, lightly beaten
1 medium onion, finely chopped
250 ml cooked *pap* (made from maize meal)
30 ml chopped fresh parsley
salt and pepper, to taste
125 ml maize meal, to coat cakes
125 ml vegetable oil, for frying
sweet chilli sauce and/or tartar sauce, to serve
4 lemon wedges, to garnish

1. Cook the potatoes in boiling water until soft. Drain well and mash them.
2. Mix the tuna, eggs, onion, *pap* and parsley into the mash.
3. Season with salt and pepper.
4. Form the mixture into 8 balls and flatten slightly to form fish cakes.
5. Coat the cakes in maize meal and refrigerate for 1 hour to set.
6. Heat a non-stick pan and add half the oil.
7. Fry 4 cakes at a time until golden brown on one side, then flip and cook the other side, and transfer from the pan onto kitchen towel.
8. Add the remaining oil to the pan, and heat and fry the other 4 fish cakes.
9. Arrange the fish cakes on a platter and serve with sweet chilli sauce and/or tartar sauce.
10. Garnish with lemon wedges.

Orange-Flavoured Butternut Soup with a Maize Meal Twist

Growing up, I never liked pumpkin, but later in life I discovered butternut, which has a nuttier taste. The first time that I tasted butternut soup, I was sold! But the soup reminded me of isijingi *(pumpkin pudding made with maize meal), and I decided to create my own version of butternut soup with a maize meal twist. This soup is best enjoyed in winter and can be frozen for up to three months.*

Serves 6

50 g butter
1 medium onion, diced
15 ml leaf masala
1 kg butternut, cubed
500 ml chicken stock
30 ml orange juice
250 ml milk
salt and pepper, to taste
60 ml maize meal
250 ml fresh cream
30 ml chopped fresh parsley, to garnish
30 ml chopped orange rind, to garnish

1. In a large saucepan with a lid, heat the butter and sauté the onion in it.
2. Add the masala and fry with the onion until lightly browned.
3. Add the butternut and sauté.
4. Add the chicken stock, orange juice and milk.
5. Season with salt and pepper.
6. Add the maize meal and stir through.
7. Cover with the lid and boil until the butternut is soft. Stir occasionally.
8. Use a stick blender (or transfer into a food processor) and blend the soup until smooth. The colour should be deep yellow and the mixture should be creamy.
9. Add 200 ml of the cream and simmer for 10 minutes.
10. Serve hot in heated bowls. Garnish each bowl of soup with a drizzle of the remaining cream, parsley and some orange rind to add the final touch and a nice twist.

Cheesy Pap Balls

Maize meal is a staple in most South African homes, and pap *balls offer a welcome variation. Instead of serving* pap *plain on a plate,* pap *balls will introduce something interesting to any lunch or dinner table. And I promise you that most guests will ask for the recipe – guaranteed.*

Makes 24

750 ml water
15 ml salt
120 g (250 ml) maize meal
30 g butter
24 x 1 cm Cheddar cheese cubes
15 ml honey
350 ml dried breadcrumbs
1 large egg, beaten
canola oil, enough for deep-frying
chutney or sweet chilli sauce, to serve

1. In a large saucepan with a lid, bring the water to a boil and add the salt.
2. Slowly add the maize meal and whisk until smooth.
3. Cook over medium heat until the right consistency is reached. The *pap* should be stiff.
4. Add the butter, and stir until mixed through and smooth.
5. Cover with the lid and take the saucepan off the stove. Set aside to cool.
6. Once cooled enough, use your hands to make balls the size of a golf ball. Insert a cube of cheese into each *pap* ball.
7. Heat the oil for deep-frying while you are rolling the balls.
8. Roll the balls in the honey and then in the breadcrumbs.
9. Next, roll the balls in the beaten egg and then again in the breadcrumbs.
10. Deep-fry the *pap* balls until golden brown. Transfer onto paper towel to drain any excess oil. Serve immediately.
11. They can be served as a snack with chutney, sweet chilli sauce, or any other sauce of your choice.

Serving suggestions

These *pap* balls form the ideal side dish and go beautifully with a *braai*. They are the perfect accompaniment to chicken, sausage and any other kind of roasted or braaied meat.

Maize Pizza

I love making my own pizza, because then I am spoilt for choice. You have complete control of every ingredient that goes into it, even every ingredient for the pizza base. We all know how kids love pizza, and this pizza recipe makes it easy to prepare with the kids helping.

Makes 2 pizza bases
Serves 4

350 g maize meal
150 g bread flour
5 g (½ sachet) dried yeast
25 g (30 ml) sugar
25 g salt
250 ml warm water
50 ml vegetable oil

Toppings
150 ml of Lucia's Tomato Sauce (see page 30)
200 g mozzarella cheese, grated or sliced
50 ml olive oil, for drizzling
fresh basil leaves

1. Preheat the oven to 180 °C.
2. In a large bowl, mix the maize, flour, yeast, sugar and salt.
3. Add the water and oil. Mix until the dough forms a ball (you may use your hands to knead or use a stand mixer).
4. Transfer the dough onto a dry, smooth surface.
5. Sprinkle with flour and knead the dough until it forms a firm ball.
6. Put the dough in a large, greased bowl and cover with cling wrap.
7. Place it in the sun or a warm place for about 1 hour to rise, until it doubles in size.
8. Dust a dry surface with flour, transfer the dough onto it, divide into 2, and roll the dough into 2 circular-shaped pizza bases.
9. Lightly grease or line a baking tray with baking paper, and place the pizza base on it.
10. Brush the pizza base with olive oil.
11. Divide the tomato sauce between the 2 pizza bases and spread evenly – leave a 2 cm border clear.
12. Bake for 4 minutes, then add half of the mozzarella.
13. Bake for another 6 minutes until the pizza base is crisp and the cheese has melted.
14. Remove from the oven and lightly drizzle with olive oil. Let it rest for 1 minute.
15. Garnish with basil leaves, and serve hot.

Flapjacks

A real treat, any time, day or night!

Makes 12

150 g flour
150 g maize meal
2.5 ml salt
5 ml sugar
5 ml baking powder
280 ml milk
1 medium egg
45 g butter, melted, plus extra for frying
bananas, sliced
strawberries
golden syrup or honey

1. In a large bowl sift the flour, maize meal, salt, sugar and baking powder.
2. Whisk together the milk, egg and butter.
3. Make a well in the middle of the dry ingredients and add the egg mixture gradually while mixing until it forms a smooth batter.
4. Heat butter in large pan over medium heat.
5. Use an ice cream scoop to spoon the batter in even amounts into the hot pan.
6. Cook each side for about 2 minutes or until golden brown.
7. Serve with bananas, strawberries and syrup.

Chocolate Brownies

Who would have thought that maize meal in brownies would work so well? This recipe makes the most moist and decadent chocolate treat. Enjoy it with whipped cream and berries.

Makes 12 brownies

80 g butter
125 ml sugar
150 g dark chocolate, chopped or broken into smaller pieces
2 large eggs
30 g (60 ml) flour
30 g (60 ml) White Star Quick maize meal
60 ml treacle sugar
60 ml sour cream
125 ml roasted walnuts, roughly chopped
12 Rolo chocolate sweets

1. Preheat the oven to 180 °C.
2. In a medium-sized saucepan over low heat, melt the butter, sugar and chocolate. Set aside.
3. In a large bowl, mix the eggs, flour, maize meal, treacle sugar and sour cream together. Fold this mixture into the chocolate mixture until well combined.
4. Fold the nuts into the batter.
5. Pour the batter into a small, flat 16 x 24 cm baking tin.
6. Imagine how you will cut the brownies into squares when baked, e.g. 4 rows of 3. Insert a Rolo in the middle of each "square".
7. Bake in the preheated oven for about 20 minutes.
8. To test, insert a skewer in the middle. If it comes out clean, the brownies are ready.

Meat Mains, Roasts and Sides

A Sunday without a hearty meat dish or at least a roast, is like a week without a Sunday – in my mind completely unfathomable! I believe Sundays are special. And when you treat something as special, it means you handle it with care because you value and treasure it.

The same goes for any meat dish. Meat is a luxury in most households in South Africa. So when I work with meat, I treat it with respect. In the same way I was taught to wear my Sunday best to church, I was also taught to put my best on my Sunday lunch table. That not only applies to the food I put on the table, but also the way in which I prepare it. To look at a dish and really notice the detail, is like seeing the evidence of that which actually cannot be seen – your heart and soul.

When you pour your heart and soul into the food you prepare, it turns into joy and pleasure. It becomes a treat for the people you share it with because they taste the love with which you prepared it. So in this chapter I would like to share with you my go-to Sunday roasts and other meat mains with which I create special spreads for the special people in my life, whether it is family and friends who take a seat at my table, or for my followers and fans who in turn use my recipes to communicate their love to their loved-ones.

I have already shared with you my Leg of Lamb with Apples recipe (see page 22) – I added the apple twist on a whim because I had apples available, and it became a family favourite. The rest of these recipes, I developed over time while I was working at *Bona Magazine* as a food editor for three months. At that stage, the task of being a food writer was a new and daunting experience, but I learned so much, in particular the ins and outs of printed media, magazines and food photography. Whenever I prepare these dishes, I am reminded of the magazine's test kitchen where I cooked and made many a happy memory with my colleagues.

Roast Chicken

Serves 6

1 whole chicken
4 sprigs rosemary, finely chopped
6 basil leaves, finely chopped
8 cloves of garlic, crushed
10 ml sea salt
15 ml freshly ground black pepper
30 g butter, melted
extra salt and pepper, to season
kitchen string or twine, to truss

1. Preheat the oven to 200 °C.
2. Pat the chicken dry with paper towel.
3. Combine the rosemary, basil, garlic, salt and pepper and mix well. Use this mixture in the next step.
4. Take the chicken's skin gently at the tip of the chicken breast, pull it slightly upward and carefully lift the skin. Then rub the herb mixture directly onto the meat under the skin.
5. Ensure that the skin is back in place and smoothed over.
6. Gently brush the melted butter all over the skin.
7. Season the skin on top with extra salt and pepper.
8. Tuck in the wings and truss the chicken with string (see tip below).
9. Place the chicken on a wire rack in a baking tin.
10. Roast in the preheated oven for about 15 minutes.
11. Reduce the heat and bake at 180 °C for another 30 to 40 minutes, until the chicken is moist inside but the skin is roasted crispy on the outside.

Tip

When roasting a whole chicken, trussing the chicken is very important to allow it to cook evenly. Truss by snugly tucking the wings and legs of the chicken as close as possible to the rest of the body, and then tie it with kitchen string to keep it compact and in place.

Beef Roast

You can't go wrong with a beef roast if you remember two golden rules: (1) Don't overcook it, and (2) most importantly, let the meat rest long enough for the meat juices to settle – this is where most people go wrong. Well-done meat loses all its flavour. Resting the meat will prevent having blood on your plate. Find the balance between these two golden rules.

Serves 4

500 g beef roast, like aitchbone
30 ml olive oil
15 ml crushed garlic
7.5 ml freshly ground black pepper
salt, to taste
Chakalaka, to serve (see page 129)

1. Preheat the oven to 200 °C.
2. Remove the roast from its packaging and immediately rinse it.
3. Use paper towel to pat the meat dry thoroughly.
4. Rub the oil all over the roast and then place the meat fat-side up on a wire rack in a roasting tin.
5. Spread the garlic evenly over the meat and season generously with salt and pepper.
6. Roast in the preheated oven for 10 minutes without opening the door.
7. Turn the heat down to 140 °C and continue roasting for another 45 minutes, or until cooked through.
8. Let it stand for 15 to 20 minutes to rest before you serve.
9. Serve with my delicious Chakalaka.

Oven-Baked Kingklip

At Bona Magazine, *I once had to prepare this dish for a photo shoot, but right before the shoot my assistant broke the fish by mistake. It was total mayhem until the photographer said, 'Don't worry, we'll cover it up.' With a huge sigh of relief, I could only marvel at the joys of technology. Kingklip is a very delicate fish and it can easily dry out, so be careful to follow the recipe.*

Serves 2

2 kingklip fillets, skin on
1 medium onion, cut in wedges
2 cloves garlic, crushed
5 ml dry oregano
1 lemon, cut into thick slices
30 ml canola oil
salt and pepper, to taste
350 g Bella or cherry tomatoes
30 m fish sauce
a handful of fresh parsley, finely chopped
4 lemon wedges, to garnish
Oven-Roasted Vegetables (see page 72), to serve

1. Preheat the oven to 180 °C.
2. In a piping-hot shallow or griddle pan over high heat, grill the fish skin until crispy.
3. Place the onion in a roasting tin. Sprinkle with the garlic and oregano. Add the lemon slices, and drizzle with the oil.
4. Season with salt and pepper. Toss to ensure the onion is coated in oil.
5. Roast for 15 minutes, turn the onion and lemon slices over and bake for 15 minutes on the other side.
6. Add the tomatoes and roast for 10 minutes.
7. Rub the fish sauce onto the fish, as well as a little oil if needed, and season with salt and pepper.
8. Place the fish on the bed of roasted onion and lemon in the roasting tin, return to the oven and bake for 10 minutes.
9. Plate the fish, garnish with parsley and lemon wedges, and serve with the roasted vegetables.

Grilled T-bone Steak with Pap Fingers and Sauce

Serves 4

4 T-bone steaks
olive oil
salt and pepper, to taste

1. Brush the steaks with oil on each side.
2. Rub salt and pepper into the steaks on each side.
3. Place the steaks in a griddle pan over high heat.
4. Grill on each side for about 3 minutes.
5. Remove from the pan and wrap in foil. Let them rest for about 5 minutes.
6. Serve with *pap* fingers and sauces (see below).

Grilled Pap Fingers with Cheese

500 ml cooked stiff *pap*
250 ml grated Cheddar cheese

1. Mix the cheese into the *pap*.
2. Grease a baking tray and evenly spread the *pap* and cheese mixture onto the tray. Refrigerate or let it stand at room temperature to set for 20 to 30 minutes.
3. Cut into fingers, and grill in a griddle pan over high heat.

Mushroom Sauce

30 g butter
½ onion, finely chopped
250 g mushrooms, chopped
3 sprigs thyme
10 ml Dijon mustard
250 ml fresh cream
salt and pepper, to taste

1. In a pan over medium heat, melt the butter and sauté the onion until translucent.
2. Add the mushrooms and thyme, and stir through.
3. Add the mustard and cream, and stir until thickened.
4. Season with salt and pepper.
5. Serve hot.

Green Peppercorn Sauce

30 g butter
½ onion, finely chopped
45 ml green peppercorns
5 g (10 ml) flour
250 ml beef stock
125 ml cream
salt and pepper, to taste

1. In a pan over medium heat, melt the butter and sauté the onion until soft.
2. Add the peppercorns and flour, and stir through.
3. Gradually add the stock while stirring until smooth.
4. Add the cream and stir through.
5. Season with salt and pepper.

Pork Belly with Crackling

This dish was introduced to me by my friend Joey, who owns a restaurant in Durban.

Serves 6

1.3 kg pork belly
5 ml sea salt
1 onion, cut into large wedges
OR 6 small onions, halved
4 carrots, washed and cut into large chunks
4 celery sticks, washed and cut into large chunks
1 bulb garlic, halved horizontally
15 ml fresh fennel
6 sprigs of fresh thyme
80 ml olive oil
250 ml white wine
30 g (60 ml) plain flour

Important: Take into account standing time in step 4.

1. Place the meat fat side up on a meat board. Pat the pork belly dry with paper towel to ensure there is no moisture, otherwise the roast will not be as crisp as it should be.
2. Score or make small incisions right through the skin over the layer of fat over the belly.
3. Rub the sea salt generously into the scored skin over the fat.
4. Leave to stand to dry for 4 hours or overnight.
5. Preheat your oven to its highest temperature.
6. Place the pork belly in a large roasting tin in the oven for about 15 minutes, or until the crackling is very crispy and golden.
7. Lower the temperature to 160 °C.
8. Place the vegetables, garlic and herbs around the pork belly in the roasting tin. Do not let it touch the crackling.
9. Drizzle the vegetables with the olive oil, again keeping clear of the crackling.
10. Cover with foil.
11. Return to the oven and continue cooking for 1 hour.
12. After an hour, carefully open the oven door and pour ¾ (180 ml) of the white wine over the vegetables. Cook for another 15 minutes.
13. Remove the roasting tin from the oven.
14. Remove the pork belly from the tin and place it on a cooling rack or wooden board to rest while you make the vegetable mash. Otherwise transfer the cooked vegetables from the tin and into a pan that you can use on the stovetop.
15. Place the vegetables in the roasting tin or pan over medium heat on the stove.
16. Add the remaining wine and flour. Stir through until thoroughly combined and the sauce starts to thicken. Simmer for 5 minutes.
17. Use a potato masher to mash the vegetables and stir until it turns into a thick-looking sauce.
18. Cook for 2 to 3 minutes over low heat. Then set aside while you cut the pork belly into slices.
19. Serve the pork belly crackling-side up with the vegetable mash.

Lemon and Garlic Lamb Chops with Sweet Potato Fries

This is my go-to recipe when I feel carnivorous and I want to spoil myself. When I was a kid, we used to eat mutton – we did not really know anything about lamb. But when I discovered lamb, I was hooked! I love my lamb chops medium-rare, and this recipe makes great leftovers. The secret is to marinade the chops overnight in lemon and garlic. Do not overcook the meat and remember to let it rest before serving.

Serves 4

6–8 lamb chops, loin or rib
45 ml olive oil
30 ml lemon juice
30 ml crushed garlic
15 ml sea salt
a pinch of black pepper
4 sprigs rosemary, chopped

1. Marinade the chops overnight in a mixture of the oil, lemon juice, garlic and salt.
2. Heat a heavy pan or skillet on the stove.
3. Place the chops in the piping hot pan, two at a time.
4. Cook for about 3 minutes on each side.
5. Remove from the stove and place the meat to rest on foil with the rosemary sprigs. Fold the foil over the chops to cover them.
6. Serve with Sweet Potato Fries (see below) or any starch of your choice.

Sweet Potato Fries

Serves 4

2 medium orange sweet potatoes, peeled
50 ml sunflower oil
flour, to dust

1. Preheat the oven to 180 °C.
2. Cut the sweet potatoes into chips.
3. Drizzle with oil and toss to cover all over.
4. Sprinkle with flour and toss to coat all over. Alternatively, put the oil-coated chips in a plastic bag, add the flour and shake the bag until the chips are completely covered in flour.
5. Place the chips on a baking tray and oven-bake for 30 to 40 minutes, or until the chips are crisp on the outside.

Oxtail Stew in Red Wine

My favourite winter dish! This dish oozes heartiness and warms the soul, especially in winter. It is a caring, sharing stew that I love to make for special friends when I have enough time on my hands. I usually serve the oxtail with dumplings, which are ideal to soak up the rich red wine sauce, but you can also pair it with pap, steamed bread, rice, couscous, polenta or mashed potatoes.

Serves 4–6

80 ml canola oil
1.5 kg oxtail
1 medium onion, roughly chopped
4 cloves of garlic, chopped
2 bay leaves
3 sprigs thyme
8–12 baby carrots
salt and pepper, to taste
1 x 400 g can chopped tomatoes
250 ml red wine
500 ml beef stock (see Lucia's Beef Stock, page 38)

1. In a large pot with a lid, heat the oil and fry the oxtail until browned on all sides. Transfer to a bowl and set aside.
2. Use the same pot to sauté the onion, garlic, bay leaves, thyme and carrots until fragrant.
3. Season with salt and pepper.
4. Add the tomatoes, and cook over low heat for about 5 minutes.
5. Add the red wine and stock, and stir through.
6. Let it simmer for about 5 minutes.
7. Add the oxtail, stir through and let it simmer over very low heat for about 3 hours or until the meat falls off the bone.
8. Serve with a starch of your choice.

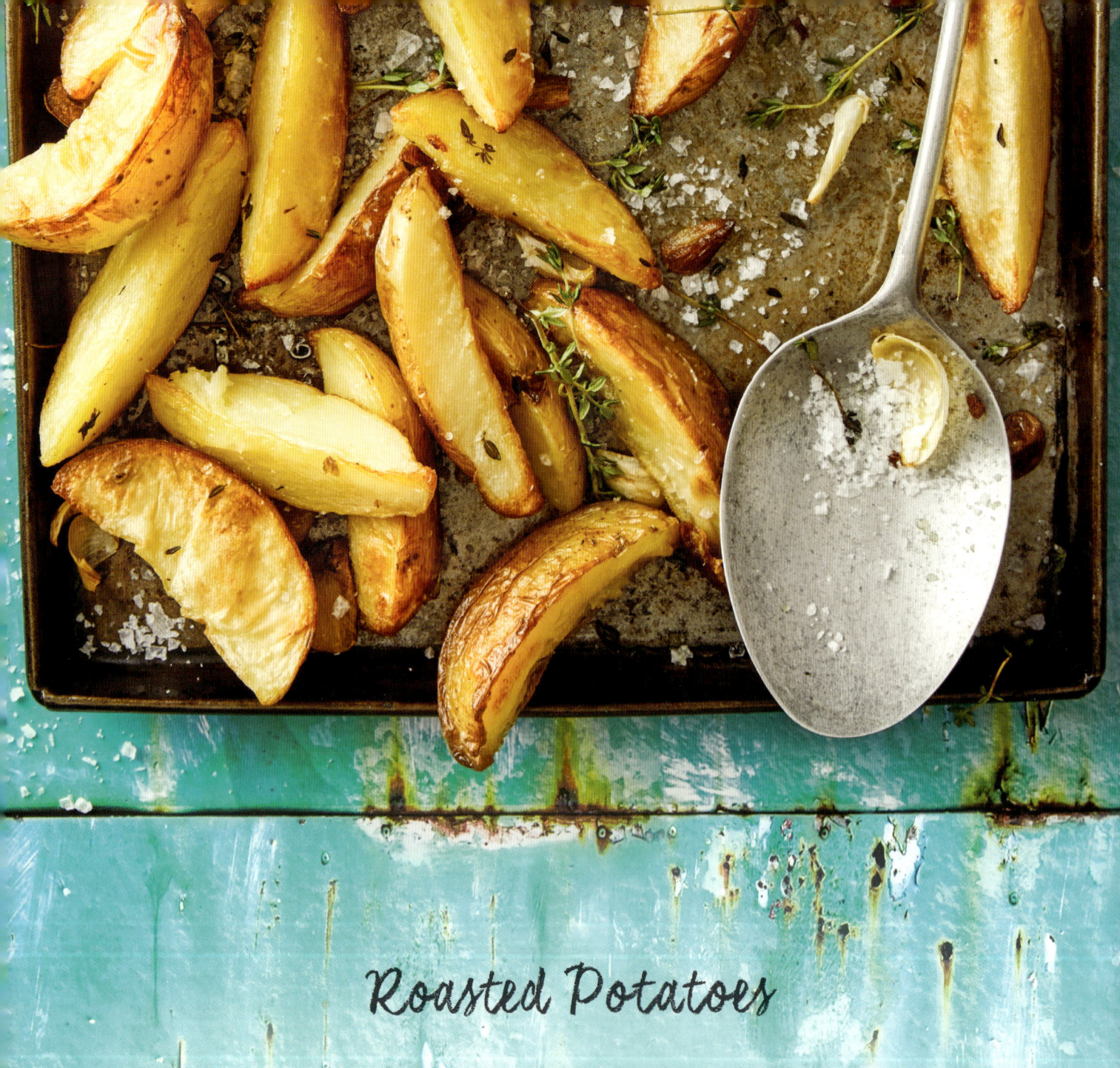

Roasted Potatoes

I cannot imagine a Sunday lunch without roasted potatoes!

Serves 6

6 medium potatoes, cut into wedges
60 ml canola oil
3 cloves garlic, sliced
3 sprigs thyme
salt, to taste

1. Preheat the oven to 180 °C.
2. Parboil the potatoes in water (just enough to cover them) for 7 to 8 minutes, and drain.
3. Use a pastry brush to generously coat the potatoes with oil and place on a baking tray.
4. Sprinkle the garlic, thyme and salt over the potatoes.
5. Roast for about 45 minutes, or until cooked through on the inside, but crisp outside.

Chakalaka

100 g butter
1 red onion, chopped
2.5 ml crushed garlic
2.5 ml grated ginger
4 red tomatoes, chopped
1 red pepper, deseeded and chopped
1 green pepper, deseeded and chopped
3 large carrots, grated or julienned
1 whole cob of corn, kernels cut off
1–2 red chillies, deseeded and finely chopped (if you like the heat, keep the seeds)
5 ml smoked paprika
5 ml masala powder

1. In a saucepan over medium heat, melt the butter and sauté the onion in it for 5 minutes.
2. Add the garlic and ginger, and fry for 1 minute.
3. Add all the remaining ingredients, and stir through.
4. Cover the saucepan and bring to a boil.
5. Reduce the heat and simmer uncovered for 15 minutes, or until cooked through.

Wheat Salad

A wholesome salad that goes well with any main dish or it can be enjoyed as a light meal on its own.

Salad
500 ml cooked wheat
1 x 250 g punnet cherry tomatoes, halved
2 celery sticks, chopped
2 spring onions, sliced
6 Peppadews, thinly sliced

Dressing
80 ml olive oil
30 ml lemon juice
50 ml chopped fresh parsley
50 ml chopped fresh basil
zest of 1 lemon
30 ml Peppadew brine/syrup

1. Combine all the salad ingredients in a salad bowl.
2. Mix together all the dressing ingredients and pour over the salad.
3. Stir through and refrigerate until needed.

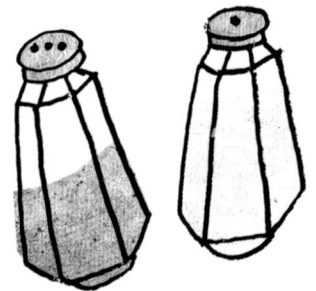

Corn on the Cob with Flavoured Butters

Serves 4

4 mealies, cooked and then grilled in a griddle pan until griddle marks appear

Flavoured butters
150 g butter, at room temperature or softened to enable mixing

Flavour 1: Sage
30 ml finely chopped fresh sage

Mix the sage into the butter. Refrigerate until needed.

Flavour 2: Anchovy and Lemon
6 anchovy fillets, finely chopped
zest of 1 lemon

Mix the anchovy and lemon zest into the butter. Refrigerate until needed.

Flavour 3: Harissa
15 ml harissa spice

Mix the spice into the butter. Refrigerate until needed.

Quinoa, Kale and Butternut Salad

During our sold-out cooking classes in Durban, my friend Tebz and I prepared this very simple quinoa salad and realised that it really is a great crowd-pleaser. It is quick to make, colourful and packed with nutrients.

Serves 6

10 ml oil
10 ml leaf masala
10 ml ground cumin
5 ml dried oregano
salt and pepper, to taste
500 g cubed butternut
2 medium baby marrows, chopped
250 ml quinoa
500 ml water
90 g chopped kale
100 ml dried cranberries
1 red onion, thinly sliced
10 ml honey
juice of 1 lemon
50 ml chopped fresh parsley OR oregano, to garnish

1. Preheat the oven to 190 °C.
2. In a medium bowl, combine the oil, masala, cumin, oregano, salt and pepper.
3. Add the butternut and courgettes, and toss to mix.
4. Line a baking tray with foil and spread the coated butternut and courgettes out on the foil.
5. Bake in the oven for 25 minutes until cooked through.
6. Remove from the oven and set aside to cool.
7. Rinse the quinoa.
8. In a medium-sized saucepan, bring the water to a boil. Add the quinoa, lower the heat and simmer for 15 minutes or until the quinoa has absorbed all the liquid.
9. Use a fork to fluff the quinoa.
10. In a large bowl, combine the quinoa, butternut, courgettes, kale, cranberries, onion, honey and lemon juice. Mix by gently stirring or tossing until well combined. If necessary, add a dash of olive oil.
11. Garnish with fresh parsley or oregano.

Outdoor and Picnic Food

When the city hustle and bustle becomes too much, and it feels as if I am suffocating in the concrete jungle I call home. I know that it is time to plan a picnic or a long, lazy lunch outside.

There is just something about being outdoors that energises, refreshes and rejuvenates body and soul – especially if you share the experience with loved ones, family and friends. And as you know by now, I believe food is for sharing, and there is just no better way to show that you care than to prepare picnic finger food or a light lunch with just as much love and attention to detail as any other meal.

My favourite time to be outdoors is in the spring. But no matter the season, when I decide to step out and connect with nature, feel the sun on my skin and the earth beneath my bare feet, I prepare my favourite nibbles and turn an ordinary outing into an extraordinary feast. Here are some of my most trusted recipes …

Sticky Chicken Wings

The ultimate picnic food, equally great as a lunchbox treat, and a winner when you need to pack finger food for a road trip. I prefer to serve them hot as a snack or starter when I am at home, but even when served cold or at room temperature, these chicken wings are a hit.

Serves 4

Chicken Wings Marinade
12–16 chicken wings
salt and pepper, to taste
125 ml plain yoghurt
15 ml paprika
15 ml masala OR medium curry powder
15 ml chicken spice

Sticky Sauce
15 ml olive oil
15 ml crushed garlic
30 ml freshly squeezed lemon juice
30 ml honey

1. Preheat the oven to 180 °C.
2. Place the chicken wings in a large bowl and season with salt and pepper.
3. Add the yoghurt and the rest of the spices. Stir through to thoroughly mix and coat, or mix with your hands until the wings are coated all over. Set aside to marinate while you prepare the sauce.
4. **For the sauce:** Mix all the ingredients together and set aside.
5. Place the wings in a roasting tin, cover with foil and bake for about 10 minutes.
6. Remove the foil, transfer the wings onto a wire rack in the roasting tin, and brush the wings on both sides with the sticky sauce.
7. Grill uncovered for 10–15 minutes, or until the skin turns crispy.
8. Remove from the oven and set aside to cool.

Pork Riblets with a Creamy Dipping Sauce

Have serviettes handy, but it is best to just lick your fingers and not waste even a drop of this dangerously delicious sticky sauce.

Serves 2

2 pork racks, cut horizontally into riblets

Riblets Sauce
salt and freshly ground black pepper
15 ml honey
125 ml mayonnaise
15 ml garlic and ginger paste
1 red onion, finely chopped
1 red chilli, deseeded and finely chopped
30 ml soy sauce
30 ml brown sugar
30 ml apricot jam

Creamy Dipping Sauce
125 ml mayonnaise
125 ml sour cream OR plain yoghurt
salt and pepper, to taste
15 ml freshly squeezed lemon juice

1. Preheat the oven to 180 °C.
2. In a medium-sized saucepan, mix all the sauce ingredients for the riblets, add the riblets and cook for about 20 minutes. Make sure the riblets are thoroughly coated while cooking.
3. Cook until the sauce becomes sticky and clings to the riblets.
4. Once cooked, transfer the riblets in its sauce to an ovenproof dish.
5. Grill in the preheated oven for another 20 minutes, or until cooked through.
6. **For the dipping sauce:** Combine all the ingredients and mix until smooth. Refrigerate until ready to serve.

Chicken Skewers

Great as a light lunch. You can add a variety of vegetables to the skewers, and the chicken can easily be replaced with beef – experiment with combinations that you like. I roast these in the oven, but also love to light a fire and put them on the braai for that added chargrilled flavour.

Makes 6–8 skewers
Serves 4–6

skewers, soaked in water if wooden

1 kg skinless, boneless chicken thighs
30 ml oil
30 ml honey
30 ml soy sauce
125 ml mayonnaise
15 ml crushed garlic
15 ml chicken spice
salt and pepper, to taste
1 red pepper, deseeded and cut into 3-cm pieces
1 green pepper, deseeded and cut into 3-cm pieces
1 yellow pepper, deseeded and cut into 3-cm pieces
oil, to grease baking tray
juice of ½ lemon
green salad, to serve
cooked couscous, to serve

1. Preheat the oven to 220 °C.
2. Cut the chicken into medium-sized pieces that will not fall off the skewers.
3. In a large bowl, whisk together the oil, honey, soy sauce, mayonnaise, garlic, chicken spice and salt and pepper.
4. Place the chicken in a medium bowl, add the peppers, and then add ¾ of the marinade (reserve ¼ of the marinade for brushing when roasting). Toss to coat the chicken and pepper pieces properly.
5. Refrigerate for at least 2 hours to marinate.
6. Remove the chicken and pepper pieces from the marinade. Discard this used marinade.
7. Thread the chicken and pepper pieces alternately onto the soaked skewers.
8. Lightly grease a baking tray with the oil, and place the chicken skewers on it. Roast for 12 to 15 minutes in the oven. Remove from the oven halfway through the cooking time, turn the skewers and brush with the reserved marinade.
9. Return to the oven and roast the other side of the skewers until cooked.
10. Serve with salad and couscous.

Meatballs with Home-Made Tomato Sauce

Nothing beats cooking a dish from scratch. Get the kids involved with this recipe, let them get their hands dirty and see the smiles on their faces when they eat what they have prepared themselves. The leftovers can be used for their lunchboxes the next day.

Serves 4

Meatballs
500 g ground beef mince
50 ml fresh breadcrumbs
1 onion, finely chopped
15 ml Worcestershire sauce
2 tomatoes, grated
1 large egg
15 ml chopped fresh parsley
salt and freshly ground black pepper, to taste

Home-Made Tomato Sauce
15 ml oil
1 onion, chopped
15 ml garlic and ginger
1 x 400 g can chopped tomatoes
5 ml sugar
15 ml dried basil
salt and pepper, to taste

1. Preheat the oven to 160 °C.
2. In a large bowl, mix all the meatball ingredients together.
3. Use a tablespoon to scoop equal portions of the mixture and roll into balls the size of a golf ball.
4. Lightly grease an overproof dish and place the meatballs in it. Spread them out evenly so that they will cook evenly.
5. Bake uncovered for about 20 minutes in the oven until lightly browned.

For the Tomato Sauce:

6. Heat the oil in a medium saucepan with a lid.
7. Add the onion and sauté until translucent.
8. Add the garlic and ginger, and stir through.
9. Add the tomatoes, sugar and basil. Stir through.
10. Season with salt and pepper, and stir through.
11. Cover and cook over low heat for about 30 minutes.

Very Versatile Wraps

Wraps are extremely versatile: you can create just about any filling by experimenting with different combinations of filling ingredients. Wraps can be served hot or cold, but taste even better when they are toasted.

Makes 10–12

360 g (750 ml) flour
5 ml salt
5 ml baking powder
80 ml canola oil
250 ml warm water

1. In a large bowl, sift the flour, salt and baking powder, and mix by stirring through with a wooden spoon. Then make a well in the centre of the dry ingredients.
2. Pour the oil and 200 ml of the water into the well, and use your finger tips to work the flour into the liquid. Add a little more water if necessary, and combine to form a dough.
3. Divide the dough into 10–12 equal-sized portions and roll into balls.
4. Place the balls on a lightly greased baking tray and let them rest for 20 minutes.
5. Dust a clean surface with flour or spray with non-stick cooking spray.
6. Use a rolling pin and roll each ball into a flat 20-cm disc.
7. Heat a large frying pan and bake the wraps in the dry pan, one at a time, on each side, until cooked and brown spots appear.
8. Set aside to cool slightly while you prepare the filling of your choice.

Filling suggestions

- Crispy or plain chicken strips + salsa / salad / roasted veggies + Lucia's Chilli Sauce (see page 33) / sweet chilli sauce / mayo / chutney
- Steak strips or Roast Beef Fillet + Chakalaka (see page 129) / salsa / salad with sweet chilli sauce / mayo / chutney
- Tuna-mayonnaise + salad
- Ham and cheese + salad + sauce of your choice
- Mini lamb meatballs + tzatziki
- Shredded smoked or plain chicken made from any leftover chicken + tzatziki or any other sauce + veg

Crispy Chicken Strips

Serves 4

500 g chicken fillets, cut into strips
60 g (125 ml) flour
2.5 ml dried oregano
2.5 ml dried mixed herbs
2.5 ml medium masala powder
salt and pepper, to taste
3 large eggs
140 g (250 ml) dried, coarse breadcrumbs
oil, for deep-frying

1. Use paper towel to pat the chicken strips dry.
2. In a medium-sized bowl, combine the flour, dried herbs, masala and salt and pepper.
3. In a separate bowl, beat the eggs until smooth.
4. Place the breadcrumbs in a separate bowl.
5. Heat the oil in a large, heavy pan over medium heat.
6. Dip the chicken strips in the flour mixture, and make sure they are covered all over.
7. Then dip them in the eggs, and make sure they are covered all over.
8. Then dip them in the breadcrumbs, and make sure they are covered all over.
9. Once the oil is hot, start frying the strips a few at a time.
10. Cook them for about 1½ minutes on each side.
11. Once golden and crispy, remove from the oil and place on paper towel to drain any excess oil.

Cheese Board

I love cheese! It instantly lifts my spirit and you will always find my fridge stocked with cheese. So it goes without saying that I am also the Queen of Cheese when it comes to creating the ultimate cheese board to round off a picnic or a long, lazy lunch outdoors.

You will need:
soft cheeses: camembert, brie, feta, Cheddar, goats' cheese, blue cheese
hard cheeses: Parmigiano-Reggiano
cream cheeses: any flavour of your choice

variety of crackers
bruschetta
cheese sticks
bread sticks

white and red seedless grapes, if in season
olives
variety of nuts, e.g. cashews
walnuts
chorizo sausage, sliced or chopped in chunks
melon slices, if in season
salami or ham
Peppadews
gherkins
berries, if in season
biltong, sliced
preserves of your choice e.g. figs

To assemble:
The difference between an average cheese board and an amazing cheese board is the correct arrangement of the delicacies on the board. My golden rule is simple: Spread the cheeses in such a manner that there is enough room to manoeuvre when cutting and dipping. Then arrange the rest of the elements to create a balanced, colourful display in such a way that everyone can reach all the elements.

Serve the nuts in separate bowls, and also be sure to separate the dairy products from the other elements in case some of your guests have allergies. Alternatively, prepare a separate snack platter for guests who might have allergies.

Cakes, Bakes and Puddings

Growing up, I had many a dream that should have seemed impossible and out of reach at the time. But so many of my dreams have come true ...

I have reached many milestones and I am proud of every accomplishment in every stage of my life thus far. Becoming a self-taught, self-made chef is by far my greatest achievement yet. However, there is one more thing that I am incredibly proud of, and that is mastering the art of baking.

Cooking is OK. But baking ... Baking is a whole new ball game. I took it upon myself to learn how to bake because, like for most people, baking is a daunting endeavour. It really is a science.

I have shared with you tips, tricks and some of my golden rules throughout this book, but now I would like to share with you a word of wisdom. Baking has taught me that if you really want to make your dreams a reality, if you really want to achieve your goals: have PASSION. It's as simple as that. Your passion will drive you, inspire you, enlighten you, and keep you going when you are struggling. Just keep on keeping on.

Practice. Every day. Work with what you have. The most basic is enough. Make it work. Until everything falls into place and you become a pro. As I have already told you, as children we siblings took turns to bake bread so that we always had home-made bread in our house. Can it get more basic than that?

Knowing that I am able to bake a decent loaf of bread gave me the confidence I needed to be bold and brave when it came to baking – in particular, when it came to a Lancewood challenge where I could have opted to cook, but I decided to bake. Lancewood asked me to enter their Social Media Baking & Cooking Competition in 2017. In this competition, we as influencers had to create a real emoji depicting either a burger, spaghetti or a birthday cake. To this day I do not know what I was thinking, but I chose the cake ... and oh boy, did I have a hard time! Baking is not my strength, but I like to push myself and my boundaries sometimes. It took me a whole week to complete the cake, but in the end my cake was voted the best and I won R20 000 worth of prizes!

In this chapter, I share with you my foolproof cakes, bakes and puddings.

Banana and Pecan Nut Loaf

I just love the crunch that the pecan nuts add to this well-known favourite.

Makes 1 medium loaf

125 g butter
200 g (250 ml) brown sugar
2 extra-large eggs
3 ripe bananas, mashed
240 g (500 ml) flour
8 g (10 ml) baking powder
a pinch of salt
100 g (250 ml) pecan nuts, chopped
banana, sliced to decorate top of loaf

1. Preheat the oven to 180 °C.
2. In a large mixing bowl, cream the butter and sugar together by whisking it until soft, creamy and smooth.
3. Add the eggs, one at a time, and mix thoroughly after each addition.
4. Stir in the mashed bananas.
5. Sift the flour, baking powder and salt together.
6. Add the dry ingredients to the banana mixture and combine well.
7. Add half the nuts and stir through.
8. Line and grease a 20 x 13 cm bread pan and spoon the mixture into it.
9. Sprinkle the remaining nuts over and decorate with half a sliced banana on top.
10. Bake in the oven for about 1 hour, or until cooked through. To test whether it is cooked, insert a skewer in the middle of the loaf – when it comes out clean, it is cooked.
11. Remove from the oven, let the loaf cool down a bit in the pan, and then turn out onto a wire rack to cool completely.

Chocolate Cake

Chocolate cake is an all-round favourite. It took me a while to finally perfect this recipe for a decadently delicious chocolate cake.

Makes 1 single-layer cake

Cake
120 g (250 ml) plain flour
210 g (250 ml) castor sugar
34 g (85 ml) cocoa powder
6 g (7.5 ml) baking powder
7.5 g (7.5 ml) bicarbonate of soda
250 ml milk
125 ml canola oil
10 ml vanilla extract
2 medium eggs
250 ml boiling water

Butter Icing
Alternative topping, or to sandwich 2 layers:
150 g butter, softened
400 g (750 ml) icing sugar, sifted
15 ml cocoa powder

Chocolate Topping
200 g white chocolate, chopped
100 ml fresh cream

1. Preheat the oven to 180 °C.
2. Grease and line a 20-cm round cake tin.
3. In a large mixing bowl, sift the flour, castor sugar, cocoa, baking powder and bicarbonate of soda.
4. Add the milk, oil, vanilla and eggs. Use a wooden spoon or an electric whisk, and beat the mixture until well combined and smooth.
5. Add the boiling water, a little at a time, and keep on mixing until smooth.
6. Transfer the batter into the tin and bake for 25 to 35 minutes.
7. Insert a sharp knife into the centre of the cake – if it comes out clean, the cake is done.
8. Remove the cake from the oven and set aside to cool completely while still in the tin.

For the Butter Icing:
9. Cream the butter and icing sugar together until well combined. Add the cocoa powder and stir together until smooth.

For the Chocolate Topping:
10. Over a double boiler or in the microwave on medium setting, add the chocolate and cream together. Stir until the chocolate melts and the mixture is smooth.
11. Set aside to cool, or until thick enough to spread over the cake.

Note

We've doubled the recipe for a double-layer cake.

To assemble:
12 Turn the cake out by first running a pallet knife around the inside of the tin to loosen the cake.
13 Single-layer cake: Spread either the butter icing or chocolate topping over the cake.
14 Double-layer cake: Spread the butter icing over one of the cake layers and transfer to a serving plate. Place the second layer of cake on top of the first layer. Use a pallet knife to spread the chocolate topping over the top layer.

Simple No-Bake Cheesecake

It does not get any simpler than this ...

Makes 1 large cheesecake

melted butter, to grease
350 g (1½ packets) ginger biscuits
30 g butter, melted
3 x 250 g bricks plain full-fat cream cheese, at room temperature
75 g (90 ml) castor sugar
45 ml fresh lemon juice
30 ml strawberry jam
raspberries and strawberries, to decorate

1. Grease a round or heart-shaped 24-cm loose-bottomed tart tin with melted butter.
2. Place the biscuits in a food processor and blitz until fine. Alternatively, put them in a plastic bag and crush with a rolling pin.
3. Transfer the biscuits into a bowl and mix with the melted butter.
4. Press the biscuit mixture firmly onto the base of the greased tart tin.
5. In a large bowl, beat the cream cheese, castor sugar and lemon juice until smooth.
6. Spoon this filling on top of the biscuit crust. Make sure it is spread out evenly. Refrigerate for 1 hour, but preferably overnight.
7. When ready to serve, remove the cheesecake from the fridge and gently remove it from the tin.
8. Spread the strawberry jam in a thin layer over the top of the cheese cake and decorate with berries.
9. Serve cold.

Malva Pudding

Serves 6

For the Pudding:
250 ml full-cream milk
5 ml bicarbonate of soda
4 g (5 ml) baking powder
120 g (250 ml) flour
140 g (175 ml) brown sugar
2.5 ml salt
1 large egg
15 ml vinegar
30 ml apricot jam

For the Sauce:
100 g (125 ml) sugar
125 ml fresh cream
125 ml boiling water
125 g butter, at room temperature
5 ml vanilla extract

1. Preheat the oven to 160 °C.
2. Mix the milk and the bicarbonate of soda together.
3. In a separate bowl, mix the remaining ingredients for the pudding.
4. Add the milk mixture to the flour mixture, and mix until it forms a smooth batter.
5. Grease an ovenproof dish of at least 5 cm deep, and pour the batter in.
6. Bake in the oven for 30 minutes, or until a skewer inserted in the middle of the pudding comes out clean.
7. Meanwhile, make the sauce by heating all the sauce ingredients in saucepan over medium heat until combined.
8. Once baked, remove the pudding from the oven. Immediately poke holes in the pudding and pour the sauce over it from the middle to the edges.
9. Let the pudding stand to soak up all the sauce.
10. Serve with Home-Made Custard (see below) or Home-Made Ice Cream (see page 162).

Home-Made Custard

As a child, home-made custard made from custard powder was not my favourite, especially when it had lumps. So I was very determined to master the art of making the perfect home-made custard from scratch. And it's true: practice makes perfect.

Serves 8

200 ml fresh cream
700 ml full-cream milk
100 g (130 ml) castor sugar
4 large egg yolks
20 g (45 ml) cornflour
5 ml vanilla extract or paste

1. In a medium-sized pot over medium heat, combine the cream and milk, but do not let it boil.
2. In a separate bowl, whisk the sugar, egg yolks, cornflour and vanilla together.
3. Transfer this egg mixture into a separate clean saucepan over medium heat. Cook while gently stirring with a wooden spoon to ensure that no lumps form.
4. Add the milk and cream mixture gradually while continuously stirring.
5. Delicious on its own, hot or cold.

Home-Made Ice Cream

This is a very popular recipe in my cooking classes. Who would have thought that ice cream is so easy to make? And you don't even need an ice-cream maker. Experiment with different flavours (see Variations below) – the possibilities are endless.

Serves 6

1 x 385 g can sweetened condensed milk
15 ml vanilla bean paste or extract
500 ml fresh whipping cream, cold

1. Pour the condensed milk into a large bowl.
2. Mix the vanilla bean paste into the condensed milk.
3. In a separate bowl, whip the cream until it forms stiff peaks – it takes about 3 minutes, or less if you use an electric mixer.
4. Scoop one large spoonful of whipped cream into the condensed-milk mixture, and gently mix.
5. Add the rest of the whipped cream and fold it in until it is smooth and silky. Make sure not to overmix as the mixture will deflate.
6. Place in the freezer until needed.

Variations: Simply add

- **PISTACHIO:** 30 g (65 ml) ground pistachio nuts per 500 ml tub of ice cream.
- **CHOCOLATE:** 12 g (30 ml) cocoa powder per 500 ml tub of ice cream.
- **LEMON & LIME:** juice of 1 medium lemon, lime and orange each + 5 ml each lemon, lime and orange rind per 500 ml tub of ice cream.
- **STRAWBERRY:** 125 g finely chopped strawberries per 500 ml tub of ice cream – add pink food colouring if you want to.
- **CHOCOLATE COOKIE:** 125 g crumbed chocolate cookies (use a food processor or place in a plastic bag and crush with a rolling pin) per 500 ml tub of ice cream.

Chocolate Ice Cream

Lemon & Lime Ice Cream

Chocolate Fondant

Again my friend Nicola, with whom I once shared an apartment, was the one to introduce me to yet another delectable dish: chocolate fondant. He really is a master when it comes to chocolate fondant, one of my sister-in-law Thandeka's favourite desserts. We would be in awe while watching him work his magic on this mouth-watering treat.

Serves 6

butter, for greasing
cocoa powder, for dusting
85 g (70 ml) castor sugar
12 g (30 ml) cocoa powder
150 g butter, softened
150 g dark chocolate, roughly chopped OR chocolate chips
3 large egg yolks
3 eggs
7 g (15 ml) plain flour
whipped fresh cream OR ice cream, to serve

1. Preheat the oven to 180 °C.
2. Grease 6 ramekins with butter and then dust with cocoa powder. Place them in the fridge for about 7 minutes while you make the fondant.
3. In a glass bowl, cream the castor sugar, cocoa and butter by whisking until smooth.
4. Place the glass bowl over a saucepan of boiling water – ensure that the bowl does not come into contact with the water. Add the chocolate or chocolate chips. Heat and stir continuously until the chocolate has melted and you have a smooth mixture.
5. Remove from the heat and set aside to cool slightly.
6. Beat the egg yolks and whole eggs, and add this mixture a little at a time to the cooled chocolate mixture – if the chocolate mixture is too hot, the eggs will curdle – and continuously stir to mix.
7. Fold in the flour.
8. Pour into the ramekins – do not fill them to the top.
9. Place the ramekins in the fridge for about 1 hour before baking.
10. Reduce the oven heat to 160 °C. Bake the fondants for 12 to 16 minutes. The fondants should still have a slight wobble in the centre.
11. Remove from the oven and immediately remove the fondants from the ramekins.
12. Serve with whipped cream or ice cream.

Yoghurt Cake

This cake is divine! Yoghurt, especially plain yoghurt, is one of the ingredients I cannot live without. Honestly, I use yoghurt or cream in just about everything. I do not have that much of sweet tooth, so I prefer to bake my own cakes, then I can control the amount of sugar that goes into them.

Makes 1 cake

Cake
180 g butter, softened
210 g (250 ml) castor sugar
4 large eggs
5 ml vanilla extract or paste
280 g (500 ml) self-raising flour
200 ml plain yoghurt
50 ml milk
100 g dark chocolate, chopped
extra 45 ml milk

Coconut Topping
100 g butter, melted
100 g (125 ml) sugar
60 ml milk
80 g (250 ml) desiccated coconut
100 ml coconut flakes
5 ml vanilla extract or paste

1. Preheat the oven to 160 °C.
2. Grease and line a 20-cm loose-bottomed or spring-form cake tin.
3. In a large bowl, cream the butter and castor sugar.
4. Add the eggs one at a time, mixing well after each addition.
5. Add the vanilla, flour, yoghurt and milk, and mix. It should not have a runny consistency, but rather be able to drip.
6. Spoon the cake mixture into the prepared cake tin.
7. In a saucepan or double boiler, melt the chocolate and extra milk together while stirring continuously until smooth. Let it cool sufficiently before you pour it over the cake batter.
8. Bake the cake in the oven for about 40 minutes or until a skewer inserted in the middle, comes out clean.
9. Remove from the oven, and allow it to cool completely on a wire rack.

For the Coconut Topping:
1. In a small saucepan over moderate heat, combine the butter, sugar and milk while stirring continuously until the sugar has dissolved. Then boil for 2 minutes.
2. Remove from the heat, and add the coconut and vanilla. Stir through well.
3. Spoon the coconut topping over the cake.
4. Place the cake under the oven grill for a few minutes until the topping turns golden brown.

Food for Body and Soul

Food equals nourishment. The secret to a healthy, nourished body and soul is to realise that body and soul are connected in everything you do. I prepare food for myself, my loved-ones, families and friends not only to nourish the body, but also to communicate that I deeply care. No amount of trouble in preparing a feast or elevating an everyday sandwich made from home-baked bread is too much when it comes to making people feel loved, nourished and nurtured.

As a singer and artist, I have also found that my soul, as well as each and every soul in my audience, needs the same amount of nourishment and nurturing. Many a day I have found strength in my music that carried me through times when I did not feel my exuberant self. Then I choose the songs that I hear my soul whispering and I turn the volume up or down accordingly.

My two greatest passions – food and music – feed my body and soul from within, but for me the nourishing qualities of food do not end there. Over the years I have learned to also value that which covers body and soul: my skin. I discovered that I can use food to also nurture the skin that I am in – the skin that keeps everything together and actually acts as the largest organ, not in my body, but of my body.

So let's look at pairing music and food to feed the soul, and finally at food solutions in taking care of your skin …

Food to feed the skin

The sense of touch is not just a sense of body, but also one of the languages of love. And each and every one of us needs to love ourselves. The sense of touch makes your skin an incredibly strong medium through which you can communicate, and on these last few pages, I show you how to take care of your skin. I share with you my recipes for skin scrubs, masks, washes and moisturisers. Please remember that skin types vary and what works for me, might not work for you. So before making and using any of my skincare recipes, consult your doctor or dermatologist if you have ever experienced or are experiencing any skin problems.

DISCLAIMER: See imprint page.

My Skincare Must-Haves

Apple Cider Vinegar

Most households swear by Apple Cider Vinegar (ACV as it is referred to by many folks) because it has external and internal uses. ACV can add shine to your hair if you apply it after shampooing. ACV can also be used on your skin as a toner. A daily shot of ACV before breakfast can boost your energy, control blood sugar levels, and will help you lose weight. I mix ACV with olive oil and drizzle it over vegetables to add flavour.

Coconut Oil

Coconut oil is excellent for cooking because it has high heat-resistance, the same as other vegetable oils. If used on your skin and hair, it helps to maintain moisture and can even help treat acne. Coconut oil can be applied directly onto your skin and hair.

Yoghurt

Yoghurt contains lactic acid, which helps reduce wrinkles and fine lines on facial skin. It also helps dissolve and remove dead skin.

Brown Sugar

Using a scrub on your face at least once a week is essential. Brown sugar is an excellent exfoliating antioxidant for your skin. It keeps your skin hydrated and locks in moisture.

Variations of Brown Sugar Facial Scrubs:

- Brown sugar and honey scrub: 30 ml sugar + 15 ml honey
- Brown sugar and olive oil scrub: 15 ml sugar + 15 ml olive oil
- Brown sugar and coffee scrub: 15 ml sugar + 15 ml coffee grounds
- Brown sugar and almond oil: 15 ml sugar + 5 ml almond oil

Rosewater

Rosewater is an essential item that I honestly cannot live without. It has a long shelf life and I find it quite reasonably priced. I have been using rosewater as a toner on my face for the past five years and the result is silky smooth, even-toned skin. Rosewater mist works well to refresh your face on a hot summer's day – simply pour rosewater into a clean spray bottle and keep it handy. It is also believed to soothe the irritation of eczema, and many people believe that rosewater has anti-ageing properties, so here is our fountain of youth, ladies! And of course I use it in cooking – I add a little to rice to make it more fragrant when cooking biryani.

Shea Butter

Shea butter is readily available and reasonably priced. It forms the basis of various types of home-made moisturisers, and in my opinion it is your skin's best friend. Shea butter is the fat extracted from the shea (karite) tree's seeds, and these trees grow wild in most parts of West Africa. It has been used to treat skin for thousands of years, and it is suitable for all skin types. What is interesting is that a shea tree can take up to 50 years to start producing shea nuts. So this is an ingredient that I treat with great respect.

A couple of years ago, my two dear friends, Matlou and Leigh Ann, introduced me to shea butter and since then it has become an integral part of my beauty regime. My family and friends call it 'women's gold' because I just cannot live without it. Ever since I started using shea butter, I have saved a lot of money on cosmetics. Shea butter has a very long shelf-life and it easily adapts to different essential oils, which makes it easy to create a variety of different flavoured moisturisers, hand creams and lip balms. You can literally use it from head to toe. It conditions and tones your skin, and it also has anti-inflammatory and healing properties, so I even use it as an aftersun home-remedy.

Turmeric Facial Mask (page 176)

Coffee Body Scrub (page 176)

Hair Treatment (page 172)

Skin and Hair Treatments

Yoghurt Facial Mask

Use this mask twice a week for glowing, healthy skin. The lactic acid in yoghurt removes dead skin cells and tightens pores, thus helping reduce fine lines and wrinkles.

60 ml plain yoghurt
15 ml olive oil

1. In a small bowl and using a fork, mix the two ingredients thoroughly.
2. Rinse your hands.
3. Use your fingertips to apply the mask to your face.
4. Leave it on for about 25 minutes.
5. Rinse the mask off with lukewarm water.
6. Pat dry and apply moisturiser (see Moisturiser, page 173).

Hair Treatment

Olive oil and egg yolk are both high in fat, and act as natural moisturisers. This treatment will strengthen and condition dry, brittle hair. I use it three times per month to keep my hair soft and moisturised.

2 medium egg yolks
30 ml extra-virgin olive oil

1. In a small bowl and using a fork, mix the two ingredients thoroughly.
2. Apply generously to your hair before washing.
3. Cover with a shower cap to keep all the moisture in.
4. Leave it on for 40 minutes.
5. Rinse your hair thoroughly with warm water, and then wash with shampoo.

My Best Facial and Neck Mask

This is a winner in winter when your skin is drier and you need to exfoliate to renew and clarify your skin.

1 medium egg, beaten
15 ml brown sugar
15 ml honey

1. In a medium-sized bowl and using a fork, mix all the ingredients until thoroughly combined.
2. Rinse your hands.
3. Use your fingertips to generously apply the mask to your face and neck.
4. Leave it on for 3 minutes.
5. Rinse the mask off with warm water. Pat dry and apply moisturiser (see below).

Moisturiser

This is the ideal facial and whole-body moisturiser. I keep a very small container of it in my handbag as hand cream. Suitable for all skin types. Replace the rosewater with any essential oil of your choice.

30 ml organic shea butter
30 ml rosewater
5 ml honey

1. In a small bowl and using a fork, mix all the ingredients into a smooth paste.
2. Rinse your hands.
3. Use your fingertips to apply the moisturiser to your face.

Variation: Hair Moisturiser

Mix equal parts shea butter and coconut oil by whisking them with a fork until fluffy, and use as a daily oil moisturiser for your hair.

Avocado Facial Mask

Growing up on a farm where we had lots of avocado trees, I learned from an early age to enjoy avo on its own, in salads or mashed, sliced or diced with a pinch of sugar (yes!), salt and pepper on white bread. One day, while I was savouring each bite of this treat, I thought: Why not treat my skin with it? And I came up with this enriching facial mask that will open up pores and leave your skin silky smooth and moisturised.

30 ml plain yoghurt
15 ml avocado, peeled and mashed
5 ml honey

1. In a small bowl and using a fork, mix all the ingredients into a smooth paste.
2. Rinse your hands.
3. Use your fingertips to apply the paste to your face. Spread evenly all over.
4. Leave it on for 10 minutes.
5. Rinse the mask off with warm water.
6. Pat dry and apply moisturiser (see Moisturiser, page 173).

Variation: Avo Hair Treatment

As hair treatment, it reduces dandruff and helps to strengthen hair by retaining moisture and therefore preventing breakage. Simply blend the ingredients into a thick paste, apply to damp hair and leave it on for 20 minutes. Rinse with lukewarm water. Then shampoo and condition as normal.

Egg and Lemon Juice Facial Mask

Lemon juice absorbs excess oils and egg white tightens pores. The combination also works well to treat pigmentation.

15 ml fresh lemon juice
egg whites from 2 medium eggs

1. In a medium-sized bowl, whisk the egg whites and add the lemon juice until well combined.
2. Rinse your hands.
3. Use your fingertips to apply the mask to your face.
4. Leave it on for 5 minutes.
5. Rinse the mask off with lukewarm water.
6. Pat dry and apply moisturiser (see Moisturiser, page 173).

Coffee Body Scrub

One of my clients gave me the best gift ever: a coffee machine for my birthday. It always broke my heart when I had to throw away coffee grounds. One day a friend of mine, Brenda Yeni, told me how I could make my own scrub using coffee grounds, and I started piling them up in my fridge. This scrub removes dead skin cells and reduces puffiness, so even while this is mainly a body scrub that reduces the appearance of cellulite, you can use it as a facial mask after a long night out, too. It leaves your skin feeling smooth and supple, and gives it a healthy glow. It keeps well in the fridge for up to a month.

150 ml coconut oil
250 ml used coffee grounds
250 ml brown sugar

1. Melt the coconut oil naturally in the sun.
2. In a large bowl and using a wooden spoon, combine the coffee grounds and sugar.
3. Add the liquid coconut oil and mix thoroughly.
4. Rinse your hands.
5. Apply generously all over your body.
6. Take a refreshing bath or shower to rinse the scrub off.
7. Gently pat your skin dry.

Turmeric Facial Mask

Turmeric has healing properties and is a staple spice in most Indian and Thai households. It has been used as a facial treatment for centuries, because it is treats acne, blackheads and blemishes. It also unclogs pores and removes excess oil from your skin. So I not only use turmeric in my curry dishes, fried rice and my Masala Mix (see page 35), I also use it to treat my skin.

15 ml turmeric powder
30 ml plain yoghurt
15 ml honey

1. In a small bowl and using a fork, mix all the ingredients into a smooth paste.
2. Rinse your hands.
3. Use your fingertips to apply the paste onto your face.
4. Leave it on for 15 minutes.
5. Rinse the mask off with lukewarm water.
6. Pat dry and apply moisturiser (see Moisturiser, page 173).

Music to soothe the soul

Music and food evoke very strong emotions. Food is a sensory experience. Sight, taste, texture and smell all come together in every bite you savour. But for the ultimate food experience, I believe in pairing food with music in order to include all five senses. Marrying the two loves of my life is a creative process in which I can get lost for hours, even days.

I remember a campaign and a particular event as part of it. I was preparing a dish with *pap* and while cooking I was practising Miriam Makeba's *Pata Pata*. To this day when I hear *Pata Pata* I still think about *pap*! There is an indescribably strong bond between music and food, and the mood and memories they create.

No matter how incredible the food, the table setting and the scene may be, if the music does not set the tone for the perfect atmosphere and ambience, any event, wedding, party or even a simple dinner will fall short and end in failure.

Most of my dishes are rustic, so jazz and the blues are the two perfect genres to pair my creations with. The minute I walk into the kitchen, the music must start playing. It stimulates and enhances my creative skills, and it simply adds something extra to each dish, but what it is, I cannot put into words.

Creamy Salmon with Pasta Rice

A sensual dish that serves two, so it is ideal for a romantic dinner. Pair it with evocative music, something to soothe both your souls and let the love you prepare it with mix with the beautiful aromas to linger in the air and create the perfect ambience.

Serves 2

2 portions salmon, skin left on
salt and pepper, to taste
20 ml vegetable oil
20 g (20 ml) butter
1 small onion, diced
4 cloves garlic, finely chopped
250 g cherry tomatoes
125 ml fresh cream
150 ml *amasi* OR plain yoghurt
500 ml baby spinach, stalks removed
36 g (100 ml) freshly grated Parmesan cheese, plus extra, to serve
20 ml chopped fresh parsley
1 x quantity of Pasta Rice (see below)

1. Season the salmon portions with salt and pepper.
2. In a medium-sized heavy pan, heat the oil and sear the salmon skin side down first, for 3 minutes. Once cooked, remove the fish from the pan and set aside on paper towel to drain any excess oil.
3. Use the same pan to melt the butter, add the onion and garlic, and season with more salt and pepper.
4. Cook while gently stirring until fragrant.
5. Add the cherry tomatoes and fry for 2 minutes.
6. Add the cream and cook over low heat while stirring.
7. Add the *amasi* or yoghurt, and stir through until thoroughly combined.
8. Season with extra salt and pepper, if necessary.
9. Add the spinach and cook it in the sauce.
10. Add the Parmesan cheese, and simmer for about 1 minute until the cheese has melted.
11. Place the rested salmon in the sauce – ensure that it is covered all over. Cook for about 1 minute.
12. Garnish with the parsley, and serve with extra Parmesan, and Pasta Rice.

Pasta Rice

Serves 2

500 ml water
200 g (250 ml) risoni pasta rice
salt, to taste
10 ml oil

1. In a medium-sized saucepan or pot, bring the water to a boil.
2. Add the pasta rice, season with salt, add the oil, and stir through.
3. Cook over high heat for about 10 minutes. Drain and rinse.
4. Serve as a side dish to a main meal.

Lamb Shanks in Red Wine

Lamb shanks in red wine: another dish I would definitely recommend for a romantic dinner, or treat your nearest and dearest with this robust, rich dish. I pair it with smooth jazzy rhythms which I turn on the minute I start cooking. Take it slow and use the long, lazy hours of cooking time to really engage with your guests.

Serves 4

4 medium-sized lamb shanks, trimmed
10 ml vegetable oil
salt and pepper, to taste, plus extra
4 sprigs rosemary
4 sprigs thyme
6 cloves of garlic
6 baby carrots
8 baby potatoes
1 large onion, roughly chopped
200 ml Lucia's Beef Stock (see page 38)
200 ml red wine of your choice – I prefer the flavour of a full-bodied merlot
10 ml cornflour (Maizena), for thickening
60 ml warm water

1. Preheat the oven to 180 °C.
2. Make 2-mm incisions all over each shank and generously rub oil, salt and pepper into the meat.
3. Heat a large griddle pan over high heat and brown the shanks on all sides.
4. Insert the rosemary and thyme sprigs into the incisions in the meat.
5. Transfer the browned shanks onto a plate and set aside to rest.
6. Line a roasting tin with heavy-duty aluminium foil.
7. Place the carrots, potatoes and onion in the tin.
8. Season generously with salt and pepper.
9. Add the stock and wine.
10. Cover with aluminium foil and roast in the oven for 3 hours.
11. Once cooked, strain all the liquid from the roasting tin into a small saucepan.
12. Return the meat and vegetables to the roasting tin, and place back in the turned-off oven.
13. Place the saucepan with the strained liquid on the stove over medium heat and cook until it reduces a little.
14. By now the garlic cloves in the roasting tin should be cooked and very soft. Squeeze them out of their skins and add to the sauce. It gives the sauce a heavenly flavour.
15. In a small bowl, add the cornflour to the water and whisk until smooth.
16. Add this paste to the saucepan and stir until the sauce has thickened and is cooked through.
17. Serve the lamb shanks and vegetables with the sauce and Steamed Bread (see page 12) that will soak up the sauce.

Watermelon and Kale Salad

This is a light and refreshing salad but can be bulked up by adding pasta rice to it (see Pasta Rice, page 179). What kind of tune would you pair this caring, sharing salad? I'd choose something with a vibe as vibrant as these ingredients.

Serves 4

Salad
500 ml chopped kale
¼ of a medium-sized watermelon, sliced
1 medium avocado, sliced – sprinkle with lemon juice to prevent it turning brown
2 wheels feta cheese, cubed
2 carrots, shaved – use a peeler to make shavings
salt and pepper, to taste
50 ml mixed seeds (optional)

Dressing
15 ml extra-virgin olive oil
10 ml freshly squeezed lemon juice
5 ml honey

1. Start assembling the salad on a large salad platter by first adding a layer of kale.
2. Next, add a layer of watermelon slices.
3. Add a third layer of avocado slices.
4. Sprinkle the cubed feta cheese over the salad.
5. Finally, sprinkle the carrot shavings on top.
6. Season with salt and pepper.
7. Sprinkle the seeds over, if using.
8. Mix all the dressing ingredients together and drizzle over the salad just before serving.

Tripe
(Mala Mogodu / Ulusu)

Sometimes all we need to strengthen us is a traditional hearty, home-made, memory-filled meal – slowly cooked to the beat of a jazzy rhythm until it reaches perfection.

Serves 6

1 kg tripe
coarse salt, to sprinkle and soak tripe
4 litres water
salt and pepper to taste
60 ml ghee OR vegetable oil
1 medium onion, roughly chopped
1 large red chilli, finely chopped
5 ml crushed garlic
10 ml garam masala
5 ml paprika
2 bay leaves
1 x 400 g can chopped tomatoes
250 ml *amasi* OR plain yoghurt, to serve
10 ml chopped fresh parsley, to garnish

1. Place the tripe in a large bowl.
2. Sprinkle coarse salt all over the tripe and add half the water.
3. Let the tripe soak for about an hour, then rinse it thoroughly under cold, running water.
4. Cut the tripe into bite-sized pieces.
5. In a large saucepan or pot with a lid, place the tripe, season with salt and pepper, and add the other half of the water.
6. Bring it slowly to a boil over low heat and cook for 3 hours or until tender. Drain and set aside.
7. In a large pan or skillet, heat the ghee or oil.
8. Add the onion and stir through.
9. Add the chilli and stir through.
10. Add the garlic and stir through.
11. Add the masala, paprika and bay leaves. Season with salt and pepper, and stir through while cooking over low heat until the onion is cooked.
12. Add the tomatoes, stir through, and cook for 2 minutes.
13. Add the *amasi* or yoghurt, and stir through.
14. The sauce should be thick by now, otherwise cook over low heat until reduced.
15. Add the tripe and cook it for about 10 minutes in the sauce.
16. Garnish with fresh parsley and serve with a starch of your choice.

Lamb Biryani

Biryani is one my all-time favourites. I grew up in Durban, renowned for its spicy food, and there I learned how tricky it can be to balance all the flavours. I compare cooking biryani to a musician composing a song, ensuring all the notes are in sync, the lyrics make sense and that it rhymes where it should.

Serves 6

500 ml basmati rice, soaked in water
10 ml rosewater OR
5 ml saffron threads OR
2.5 ml turmeric powder
salt
20 ml biryani mix (the one with whole spices, i.e. star anise, cloves, cinnamon sticks, etc.)
2 medium tomatoes, grated
125 ml plain yoghurt
10 ml ground coriander
1 kg lamb pieces
20 ml vegetable oil
20 ml ghee
1 medium onion, chopped
10 ml masala powder
10 ml ground cumin
5 ml turmeric
1 red chilli, halved lengthways
10 ml garlic and ginger paste
150 ml boiling water
10 g tomato paste
125 ml lentils, cooked
15 ml chopped fresh coriander

1. Cook the basmati rice as per the packet instructions, but only halfway. It must not be fully cooked.
2. Add the rosewater, saffron or turmeric, and stir through.
3. Season with salt to taste, and set aside.
4. In a large bowl, combine the biryani mix, tomatoes, yoghurt and coriander. Marinate the lamb in this mixture.
5. In a heavy pan or skillet over medium heat, heat the oil and ghee together.
6. Add the onion and fry for a few seconds. Add the masala, cumin, turmeric, chilli, garlic and ginger paste, and stir through.
7. Add the marinated lamb, as well as a little bit of water, and cook. As soon as it looks like anything is sticking to the bottom of the pan, add a bit more water.
8. Once the lamb is cooked on all sides and the water reduced, add the tomato paste and stir through.
9. Add the lentils and half-cooked rice in a layer on top of the lamb.
10. Let it steam over very low heat for 2 hours. Do not mix it – keep it in layers.
11. Garnish with freshly chopped coriander and serve.

Tips & Variations

- The lamb can be replaced with any meat of your choice.
- Some people prefer baking the dish, but you need to keep a very close eye on it to ensure it does not dry out or burn onto the bottom of the ovenproof dish.
- I prefer cooking biryani on the stovetop, because that is how my friend and very passionate cook Lerato, whom we fondly call Lele, does it. She shared her recipe with me, and I added a few twists and turns to make it my own, for example, adding rosewater or saffron. Be creative and experiment like I did. Just remember that the flavours should balance each other.

Acknowledgements

I am the woman I am today because of the Man Above: Thank You for listening to my prayers and giving me strength.

To my late mother Catherine: thank you for encouraging us to follow our dreams.

To my siblings Ntobeko (and your husband Elphas), Thuli, Senzo (and your wife Selu), Sandile (and your wife Thandeka): I draw strength and inspiration from the firm foundation you give me to build on. You are the best siblings and in-laws I could ever ask for.

Thank you to everyone from the Umzinyathi District: you are my heart and soul. To all my uncles, aunts and cousins: I love you dearly.

To all my nieces and nephews: thank you for being my guinea pigs!

To my publisher Lindy: thank you for believing in me and for the positive pressure that gently pushed me closer to achieving greatness. I could not have done it without you and your team. To my editor Nelani: thank you for streamlining my text and putting my thoughts and feelings into words so accurately. Tani, thank you for cooking up a storm, recreating my creations, and testing each and every single recipe. Melodie, thank you for the numerous cups of coffee with which you kept us going and for doing all the dishes afterwards! Hannes, thank you for the stunning illustrations and styling. Henk, thank you for capturing my creations on camera – the photography is absolutely phenomenal. Kate, thank you for helping Henk and checking that the focus on all the images was always on point. Wilna, thank you for taking all of the above and weaving it together within an incredibly beautiful design and page layout. Christine, for letting us use your beautiful home for the shoot, thank you.

Lele, thank you for all the cooking tips, and thank you for always listening whenever I needed an ear.

Matlou, Leigh-Ann, Lisa, Tumi and Craig Jacobs, you have encouraged me to be the best version of myself. You form part of the foundation of this book – thank you.

Brenda and Theo, thank you for always believing in me and my ability to build a strong brand based on my passion for food. I appreciate you, my friends.

Thobile, my sous chef, thank you for your hard work.

And finally, to all my fans and followers, other family and friends, chefs and colleagues: you impact and inspire me from one day to the next – THANK YOU! All of you continuously encourage me to keep on dreaming and pursuing my goals.

I appreciate you beyond measure.

All my love,
Lucia

Index

A
All-Day Breakfast 98
amasi (sour milk/cream) 25, 28, 77
Anchovy and Lemon Flavoured Butter 133
apple cider vinegar (ACV) 171
apples 22
asparagus 10, 70
Avo Hair Treatment 173
Avocado Facial Mask 175

B
baby marrows 10
bacon 14, 48
baking 110, 153
Banana and Pecan Nut Loaf 154
bananas 108, 154
basmati rice 28
beans
    all-day breakfast 98
    black beans 88
    green beans 10, 67, 70
    kidney beans 88 a
    three-bean curry 88
    tinned or dry 28
beef
    curry 82
    fillet 68
    meatballs 90, 144
    oxtail 127
    roast 116
    stock 38
    T-bone steak 120
Beef Curry with Jasmine Rice 82
Beef Fillet, Roast 68
Beef Roast 116
Beef Stock, Lucia's 38
beetroot 62, 72
Beetroot Salad 62
berries 58, 75, 108, 110, 134, 150, 159, 164
Biryani, Lamb 186
black beans 88
bread
    banana 154
    crumbs 28
    maize 15
    panko 28
    spinach 43
    steamed or baked 12
Bread, Steamed or Baked 12
Breakfast, All-Day 98
broccoli 10
Brown Sugar Facial Scrubs 171
butter 28
    flavoured 133
Butter Chicken a.k.a. *Murgh Makhani* **95**
Butter Icing 154
butternut 46, 62, 72, 102, 134

Butternut Pie 46
Butternut Salad, Quinoa, Kale and 134
Butternut Soup with a Maize Meal Twist, Orange-Flavoured 102
Butternut, Grilled 62

C
cabbage 50, 65
cakes 153, 154, 166
Cakes, Bakes and Puddings 153
Cape Salmon 92
Chakalaka 129
Cheddar cheese 105, 120, 150
Cheese Board 150
Cheese Cake, Simple No-Bake 159
Cheese, Grilled Pap Fingers with 120
Cheesy Pap Balls 105
chick peas 88
chicken (*umleqwa*) 54
    butter chicken 92
    curry 80
    hand-raised Zulu 54
    roast 115
    skewers 142
    sticky wings 138
    strips, crispy 149
    truss 115
Chicken Curry 80
Chicken Skewers 142
Chicken Strips, Crispy 149
Chicken Wings, Sticky 138
Chicken, Roast 115
Chilli Sauce (Jalapeño), Lucia's 33
chocolate 110, 154, 162, 164
Chocolate Brownies 110
Chocolate Cake 154
Chocolate Fondant 164
Chocolate Topping 154
chorizo 43, 150
cinnamon 36, 46
coconut oil 171
Coconut Topping for Yoghurt Cake 166
Coffee Body Scrub 176
Coleslaw 50
condiments 24
convection oven 8
coriander 28, 36
corn
    chakalaka 129
    on the cob 133
corn flour (for thickening) 28
Corn on the Cob with Flavoured Butters 133
Crackling, Pork Belly with 122
cream, fresh 28
Creamy Dipping Sauce, Pork

Riblets with a 141
Creamy Salmon with Pasta Rice 179
Crispy Chicken Strips 149
cumin 36
curry 21, 77
    beef 82
    butter chicken 95
    chicken 80
    crisis 21
    fish 92
    in-a-hurry 21
    lamb 78
    leaves 28
    meatballs 90
    mince 87
    prawn 57
    sauce 90, 92
    three-bean 88
    tamarind 92
Curry Mix, My Best Basic 35
Curry Queen 77
Curry Sauce, Meatballs in a 90
Curry, Beef 82
Curry, Chicken 80
Curry, Mince 87
Curry, Prawn 84
Curry, Tamarind Fish 92
Curry, Three-Bean 88
Curry, Yoghurt and Cream Lamb Curry 78
Custard, Home-Made 160

D
danya 78
Dry Masala Powder Mix 36

E
Egg and Lemon Juice Facial Mask 176
egg yolk powder 70
eggs in fried rice 70

F
Facial and Neck Mask, My Best 173
Facial Mask, Avocado 175
Facial Mask, Egg and Lemon Juice 176
Facial Mask, Turmeric 176
Facial Mask, Yoghurt 172
Facial Moisturiser 173
Fillet, Roast Beef 68
fillings for wraps 146
finger food 137
Fish Cakes, Maize Meal 100
Fish Curry, Tamarind 92
Fish Dish, My Go-To / Tinned Fish Curry 21
fish
    Cape Salmon 92
    curry 21
    fish cakes 100

Kingklip 118
pre-cooking 92
Tilapia 92
tuna 100
Flapjacks 108
flavoured butters: sage, anchovy and lemon, harissa 133
flour 28
Fondant, Chocolate 164
Food for Body and Soul 169
Food I Grew to Love, The 41
Food to Feed the Skin 169–176
Fried Turmeric Rice 70
fries, sweet potato 124

G
garam masala 35
gelatine powder 28, 58
ghee 28
green beans 10, 67, 70
Green Beans 67
Green Peppercorn Sauce 120
green vegetables 10
Grilled Butternut 62
Grilled Pap Fingers with Cheese 120

H
Hair Moisturiser 173
Hair Treatment 172
Hair Treatment, Avo 173
Happiness is Home-Made 12
hard-body chicken 54
Harissa Flavoured Butters 133
home-made bread 12
Home-Made Custard 160
Home-Made Ice Cream 162
honey 28

I
Ice Cream, Home-Made 162
pistachio, chocolate, lemon and lime, strawberry, chocolate cookie 162
idombolo (dumpling) 12
isijingi (pumpkin pudding made with maize meal) 102

J
jalapeños 33
Jasmine Rice 82
jelly *see* trifle

K
Kale and Butternut Salad, Quinoa 134
Kale Salad, Watermelon and 182
Kashmiri chilli powder 21
kidney beans 88
Kingklip, Oven-Baked 118

L
lamb 22, 78, 124, 180, 186
Lamb Biryani 186
Lamb Chops, Lemon and Garlic 124
Lamb Curry, Yoghurt and Cream 78
Lamb Shanks in Red Wine 180
Leg of Lamb with Apples 22
Lemon and Anchovy Flavoured Butter 133
Lemon and Garlic Lamb Chops with Sweet Potato Fries 124
lemon and lime ice cream 164
Lemon Juice and Egg Facial Mask 176
lemon juice tip 50
Loaded Bacon and Potato Skins 48
Lucia's Béchamel Sauce 16 *also see* 15
Lucia's Tomato Sauce 30

M
macon 16
madumbes (yams) 7
mainstay recipes 7
maize 25, 28
   bread 15
   recipes 97–111
   also see pap
Maize Meal and Flour Bread 15
Maize Meal Fish Cakes 100
Maize Meal Twist, Orange-Flavoured Butternut Soup with a 102
Maize Pizza 106
Maize Starz 97
***Mala Mogodu* (Tripe) 184**
Malva Pudding 160
mango 57
marinade
   butter chicken 95
   chicken skewers 142
   lemon and garlic lamb 124
   sticky chicken wings 138
masala 28, 34
Masala Mixes 34
   basic curry 35
   dry 36
   wet 36
masks *see* skin and hair
meat 113 *also see* beef, bacon, chicken, lamb, mince, pork, sausage, T-bone steak
Meat Mains, Roasts and Sides 113
Meatballs in a Curry Sauce 90
Meatballs with Home-Made Tomato Sauce 144
micro-greens 10
Microwave Greens 10

mince 30, 87, 144
Mince Curry 87
Moisturiser 173 *also see* skin and hair
mozzarella cheese 106
Murgh Makhani, Butter Chicken a.k.a. 95
Mushroom Sauce 120
mushrooms 70
mustard 120

N
Neck Mask, My Best Facial and 173

O
olive oil 28
onion powder 28
Orange-Flavoured Butternut Soup with a Maize Meal Twist 102
oregano 28
Outdoor and Picnic Food 137
Oven-Baked Kingklip 118
Oven-Roasted Vegetables 72
Oxtail Stew in Red Wine 127

P
panna cotta 58
Pantry Staples 27
pap (maize) 8
   balls 105
   fingers 120
   staple 28
   tricks 98
   also see maize
Pap Balls, Cheesy 105
Pap Fingers and Sauce, Grilled T-bone Steak with 120
Pap Fingers with Cheese, Grilled 120
Parmesan cheese 98
parsley 28
pasta 8, 16, 179
Pasta Debut, My 16
Pasta Rice 179
Pasta with Bacon-Wrapped Pork Bangers 16
Pecan Nut Loaf, Banana and 154
Peppercorn Sauce, Green 120
picnic food 137
pilchards 21
Pizza, Maize 106
plain yoghurt 28
pork
   bangers 16
   ham 150
   pork belly with crackling 122
   riblets 141
   also see bacon
Pork Belly with Crackling 122
Pork Riblets with a Creamy Dipping Sauce 141
Potato Skins, Bacon and 48

potatoes 8
　potato skins 48
　roasted 72, 128
Prawn Cocktail 57
Prawn Curry 84
pre-cooking fish 92
pudding 58, 75, 108, 110, 153
pumpkin 46 also see butternut

Q
queen
　curry 75
　kitchen 5–6, 25
Quinoa, Kale and Butternut Salad 134

R
Rainbow Trifle 75
riblets, pork 141
rice 8
　basmati 28
　fried 70
　jasmine 28, 82
　pasta 179
　turmeric 70
Rice, Jasmine 82
Rice, Pasta 179
Roast Beef 116
Roast Beef Fillet 68
Roast Chicken 115
Roasted Potatoes 128
Roasted Vegetables, Oven- 72
roasts 113
rosemary 28
rosewater 171

S
Sage Flavoured Butter 133
Salad Dressing 182
salad
　watermelon and kale 182
　wheat 130
Salad, Watermelon and Kale 182
Salmon with Pasta Rice, Creamy 179
samp 53
Samp and Beans 53
Sandwiches
　bread 12, 15, 21
　fillings see wraps
sardines 21
sauce
　creamy dipping 141
　green peppercorn 120
　mushroom 120
　riblets 141
　sticky wings 138
　tomato 30, 144
sausage 98
　chorizo 43, 150

pork bangers 16
scrubs see skin and hair
seafood see Cape Salmon, fish, Kingklip, prawns, Tilapia, tuna
Seven Colours 61
　Sunday lunch 7
shea butter 171
sides 113
　chakalaka 129
　corn on the cob 133
　flavoured butters 133
　pap fingers 120
　oven-roasted vegetables 72
　roasted potatoes 128
　sweet potato fries 124
　watermelon and kale salad 182
　wheat salad 130
　also see rice, sauces
Simple No-Bake Cheese Cake 159
Skewers, Chicken 142
skin and hair care treatments
　disclaimer 2
　must-haves 170
　scrubs, masks, washes, moisturisers 172–176
skin see Food for Body and Soul, Food to Feed the Skin
snacks 48 also see outdoor and picnic food
Spinach Bread (*ujeqe*), Steamed 43
spinach or *morogo* 43, 44
Spinach with Chorizo Sausage 43
staples 27
starch 8 also see pap, pasta, rice, potatoes
startle-steam 8
steak see beef
Steak with Pap Fingers and Sauce, Grilled T-bone 120
steam, startle- 8
Steamed Spinach Bread (*ujeqe*) 43
Sticky Chicken Wings 138
Sticky Sauce 138
stock, beef 38
strawberries see berries
sugar 28
Sweet Potato Fries 124

T
T-bone Steak with Pap Fingers and Sauce, Grilled 120
Tamarind Fish Curry 92
Three-Bean Curry 88
thyme 28, 68
Tilapia 92
tinned fish 21
tomato sauce 30, 144
　tinned 28
treatments see skin and hair

Trifle á la Lucia 58
Trifle, Rainbow 75
Tripe (*Mala Mogodu / Ulusu*) 184
tuna 100
turmeric 28, 35
Turmeric Facial Mask 176

U
ujeqe (steamed bread) 12
Ulusu (Tripe) 184
uphuthu (dry pap) 25

V
vanilla extract or paste 28, 46
vegetable oil 28
vegetables
　oven-roasted 72
vinegar 28

W
washes see skin and hair
Watermelon and Kale Salad 182
Wet Masala Paste Mix 36
What is in a Name 6
Wheat Salad 130
White Cabbage 65
wraps and fillings 146
Wraps, Very Versatile 146

Y
yeast 28
yoghurt 171
Yoghurt and Cream Lamb Curry 78
Yoghurt Cake 166
Yoghurt Facial Mask 172

Z
Zulu Chicken 54
Zulu girl 25